Connecting Pentatonic Patterns

THE ESSENTIAL GUIDE FOR ALL GUITARISTS

BY TOM KOLB

To access audio visit:
www.halleonard.com/mylibrary

Enter Code
1216-8644-2852-3579

ISBN 978-1-4234-9628-1

HAL•LEONARD®
CORPORATION
7777 W. BLUEMOUND RD. P.O. BOX 13819 MILWAUKEE, WI 53213

In Australia Contact:
Hal Leonard Australia Pty. Ltd.
4 Lentara Court
Cheltenham, Victoria, 3192 Australia
Email: ausadmin@halleonard.com.au

Visit Hal Leonard Online at
www.halleonard.com

CONTENTS

ABOUT THE AUTHOR

A veteran of over 7,000 live performances and recording sessions worldwide, Tom Kolb has found himself in just about every musical situation imaginable. He currently maintains a busy schedule of gigs and sessions with a wide variety of artists in the Los Angeles area and abroad, including his own band, the Gurus.

An instructor at the world-famous Musicians Institute (G.I.T.) since 1989, Tom has authored seven instructional books—*Soloing Strategies, Music Theory for Guitarists, Chord Progressions, Modes for Guitar, All About Guitar, Amazing Phrasing,* and *Daily Guitar Warm-Ups*—and has been the featured artist in a wide variety of instructional guitar DVDs and videos, including *Melodic Lead Guitar, 50 Licks Rock Style, Famous Rock Guitar Riffs and Solos, Fender Stratocaster Greats, Modes for the Lead Guitarist, Starter Series (Volumes 1 & 2), Best of Lennon and McCartney for Electric Guitar,* and the *Hal Leonard Guitar Method.* All books and videos are available through Hal Leonard. Tom also has a series of downloadable instructional videos available at *GuitarInstructor.com.*

In addition to authoring method books, Tom has written countless magazine articles for *Guitar World, Guitar Edge,* and *Premier Guitar,* and was an associate editor and a monthly columnist for *Guitar One* magazine from 2001 to 2007. You can contact Tom at his website, *TomKolb.com.*

ACKNOWLEDGMENTS

I'd like to thank my wife, Hedy, and my daughter, Flynnie, for their unconditional love and support; Hal Leonard Corporation; Bruce Atkinson, for the brilliant bass playing on the audio tracks; all my guitar heroes; and the amazing musicians who I have had the privilege of playing with over the years.

INTRODUCTION

Name a famous rock guitar solo and chances are good that the minor pentatonic scale provides its foundation. It is for this very reason that many budding lead guitarists cut their soloing teeth on the minor pentatonic scale. The sad part, though, is that too many of these players rely too heavily on one pattern (or position), either afraid or unable to skirt its boundaries and venture into uncharted territories.

If you've been finding yourself trapped in the pentatonic box, then this book is for you! Although geared toward the intermediate guitarist, the book offers examples for players of all levels, from beginner to advanced. The only prerequisites are a basic understanding of the minor pentatonic scale and a desire to expand your fretboard horizons. Study this book faithfully, and soon you'll be soloing all over the neck with the greatest of ease.

HOW TO USE THIS BOOK

Divided into chapters, *Connecting Pentatonic Patterns* explains in detail the five pentatonic patterns and how to connect them to create seamless solos. The text explores a wide variety of improvisational concepts and techniques, backed with exercises and lick examples galore! In addition, Chapters 1–4 include two extended solos paced at two skill levels—one on the easier side and one more advanced. Chapter 5 contains four solos in various keys, Chapter 6 contains three solos based on the major pentatonic scale, and Chapter 7 contains two solos that mix and combine major and minor pentatonic scales. The solos themselves are played in rock, blues, funk, and country styles, and are based entirely on the techniques presented in each lesson. Furthermore, most chapters feature a "Quick Theory Tutorial" that you can refer to if you need to brush up on your music theory. You'll also find a section called "Tone Tips," which precedes each solo. Here, you'll find suggestions for guitar, amp, and effects settings. To top it all off, Chapter 8 contains a variety of play-along tracks that you can jam along with, complete with chord charts and soloing suggestions.

I sincerely hope this book helps you on your musical quest for fretboard freedom.
—*Tom Kolb*

Suggested companion books:
Music Theory for Guitarists, *Modes for Guitar*, *Soloing Strategies*, and *Amazing Phrasing*, all available through Hal Leonard.

ABOUT THE RECORDING

All of the music examples in this book are performed on the accompanying audio tracks. To locate the appropriate audio example, simply match the track number indicated in the text with the audio track number. Some tracks include two or more performances. In these cases, the audio icon includes "minutes and seconds" information, which indicates where each example is located within the track.

In the extended-solo tracks, the lead guitar is mixed hard-right (right side of your stereo system), with the backing instruments mixed hard-left. This enables you to isolate the guitar example by adjusting your balance control to the right, eliminating (or diminishing) the volume level of the backing instruments. You can also dial out the lead guitar by setting the balance to the left. That way, you can play along to the rhythm track without the interference of the featured guitar. (If your system doesn't have a balance control, you can isolate either side by disconnecting one of the speakers. If you're using headphones or earphones, simply remove either the left or the right side from your ear.)

Musicians:

Tom Kolb: guitars, keyboards, and drum programming
Bruce Atkinson: bass guitar

TUNING NOTES

Listen to Track 1 for tuning reference notes. Each string is played three times.

 TRACK 1

CHAPTER 1

PENTATONIC SCALE APPLICATIONS:
Pattern 1 and Extension Boxes

This chapter serves as an introduction to the "primary" pattern of the minor pentatonic scale and its two "extension boxes." (Note: many terms, techniques, and phrasing ideas are introduced in this chapter. Therefore, it contains more text and examples than subsequent chapters.) Included in this chapter are "lick" examples drawn from the pattern, scale-sequencing concepts, legato techniques, and rhythmic phrasing ideas. As with all subsequent chapters, there are extended solo demonstrations that utilize the examples presented in the text.

The A Minor Pentatonic Scale: Pattern 1

Fig. 1 shows a two-octave pattern of the A minor pentatonic scale (A–C–D–E–G) as it appears on the music staff (top staff) and the tablature staff (bottom staff). (Refer to the Guitar Notation Legend on page 143.) The numbers below the tab staff represent fret-hand fingering suggestions. Fret-hand fingering is a crucial factor in successfully connecting pentatonic patterns along the neck. (Listen to Track 2 to hear a demonstration of the example.)

Fig. 2 on the next page shows neck diagrams. These three diagrams illustrate the A minor pentatonic scale as it appears on the fingerboard. Notice that the first diagram uses dots (roots are circled) to depict the notes. The use of dots rather than note names allows for easy transference to other areas of the neck for transposition purposes. For example, slide the entire pattern up to the eighth fret and you would have the C minor pentatonic scale (C–E♭–F–G–B♭). Slide it down to the third fret and you'd get the G minor pentatonic scale (G–B♭–C–D–F). (For the sake of continuity and clarity, this book will concentrate chiefly on the A minor pentatonic scale.)

There are five patterns (positions) of the pentatonic scale on the guitar neck. Of the five, this particular scale pattern is often referred to as the "primary" pentatonic box. It is the most common pattern of the minor pentatonic scale, and throughout this book it will be referred to as "Pattern 1."

TRACK 2

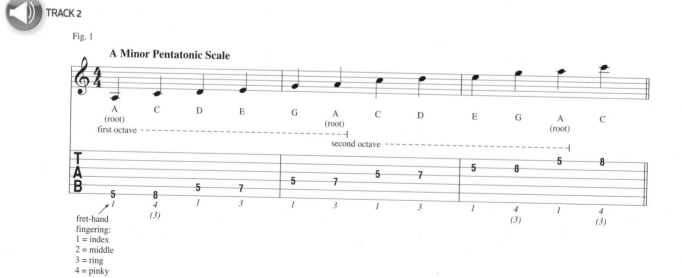

Fig. 1

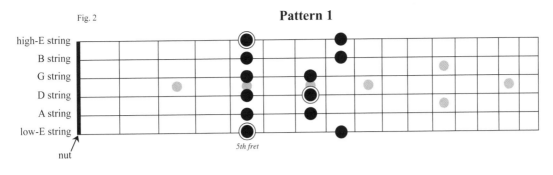

Fig. 2   **Pattern 1**

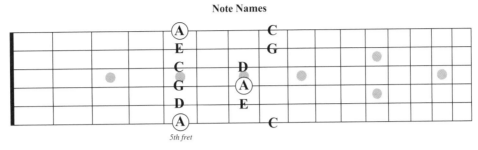

Note Names

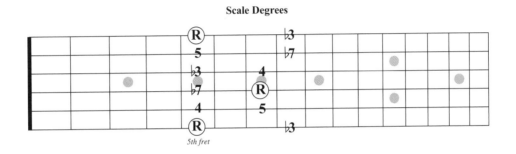

Scale Degrees

Pattern 1 Licks

Next are some lick examples crafted from Pattern 1. These phrases serve as an introduction to some of the techniques that will be used throughout the book. Although they can be used in other circumstances (which I'll explain later), the licks are all well-suited for an Am (A–C–E) or A5 (power chord: A–E) harmony.

As an added bonus, each lick includes a brief description of the guitar tone used: pickup selection (neck, bridge, middle, or combination); pickup type (humbucker or single coil); and amount of overdrive (clean, light overdrive, medium overdrive, etc.). Unless otherwise notated, assume the amplifier tones are "flat" (treble, middle, and bass are all halfway up).

Legato, Vibrato, and Percussive Techniques

Fig. 3A demonstrates how a little bit of rhythm can add interest to a simple scale ascension. A few important techniques are worth noting here: first is the "dead note" in measure 1. This is a percussive technique that is achieved by striking the string while the fretting finger (or fingers) mutes the same string. Also take notice of the little dots above and below some of the note heads in measure 2. These are *staccato* symbols and indicate that the notes are played shorter than their full values. The symbols above the tab staff are picking-direction suggestions.

Quick Theory Tutorial #1

The *minor pentatonic scale* is essentially a streamlined version of the *natural minor scale*. Whereas the natural minor scale contains seven notes, the minor pentatonic scale contains five. For example, the A natural minor scale is spelled: A–B–C–D–E–F–G. The A minor pentatonic scale omits the second and sixth scale tones, B and F, resulting in a five-note scale: A–C–D–E–G. Theoretically, this two-note exclusion omits the "awkward" half-step intervals (the space of one fret) between the second and third and the fifth and sixth scale tones. On the fretboard, this translates to finger-friendly two-notes-per-string scale patterns.

In music theory, scales are often defined as numeric formulas. For example, the formula for the major scale is: 1–2–3–4–5–6–7. All other scales are described as how they compare to the major scale. For instance, the natural minor scale differs from the major scale in that the third, sixth, and seventh scale tones are lowered by a half step. Therefore, its formula reads: 1–2–♭3–4–5–♭6–♭7. The "♭" symbol stands for "flat," or lowered by half a step. Since the minor pentatonic scale omits the 2nd and ♭6th of the natural minor scale, its formula reads: 1–♭3–4–5–♭7.

Connecting Pentatonic Patterns

Picking-direction choices vary from player to player, so feel free to experiment with other options. For instance, the *pull-off* in measure 2, whereby the fretting-hand finger sounds the note by "pulling off" from the string with a slight plucking motion, is purely a matter of taste. Feel free to replace it with a pick attack. The fret-hand fingering suggestions below the tab staff should also be taken with a grain of salt. These are logical suggestions but, again, they are not written in stone! Lastly, don't overlook the fret-hand *vibrato* markings (the squiggly lines above the staves). These are generally applied to sustained notes to give them life. Feel free to use either a classical vibrato (side-to-side motion) or a blues-rock vibrato (rapid, up-and-down bending motion). If your guitar is so equipped, you can even use the whammy bar. And don't forget, all of the examples in this book are demonstrated on the accompanying audio. Listening to the examples is the best way to get the true intent, feel, and tone of each phrase.

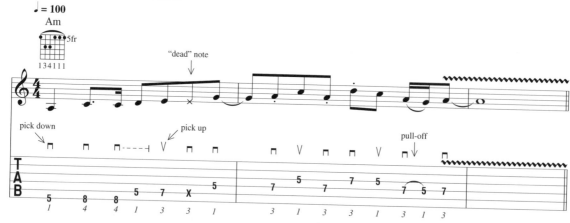

Fig. 3A (bridge humbucker; medium overdrive)

The next two examples are descending licks. **Fig. 3B** is simple but soulful, while **Fig. 3C** ups the ante with a succession of rapid pull-offs. Again, feel free to experiment with picking options rather than going with the legato notation.

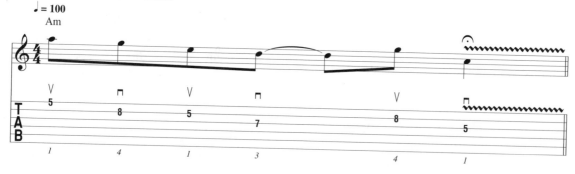

Fig. 3B (neck humbucker; medium overdrive)

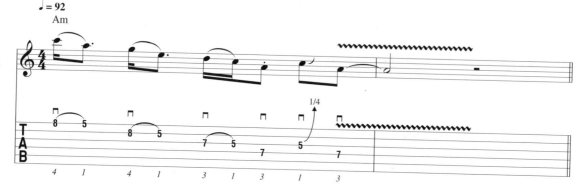

Fig. 3C (neck humbucker; light overdrive)

Fig. 3D is a meaty, blues-rock phrase concentrated on the lower string set. The rapid delivery of the 16th-note triplets (three 16th-note attacks in the space of two) in measure 1 calls for a hammer-on/pull-off ("hammer/pull") maneuver: keeping your index (1st) finger in place at the fifth fret, slam your ring (3rd) finger down hard on the seventh fret of the D string, then quickly pull off to sound the note that your index finger is holding at the fifth fret. The palm-muted notes (lightly rest the heel of your picking hand against the strings, just above the bridge of the guitar) give the phrase a chunkier texture.

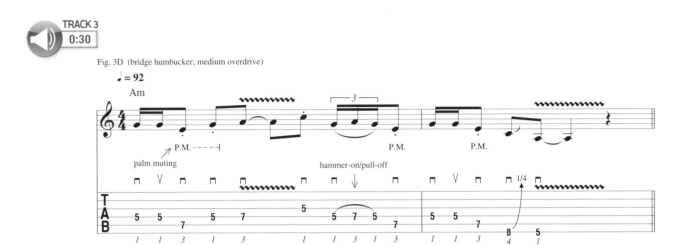

Fig. 3E opens with a hammer/pull move, followed by a bluesy quarter-step bend, also called a "microtone bend." (The fretted note is raised in pitch by bending the G string up slightly with the fretting finger.) The subtle bending of the ♭3rd of the minor pentatonic scale (in this case, C) is common practice in blues, rock, and country styles. Not quite a half step (which would result in a major 3rd), the quarter-step bend results in an edgy sound.

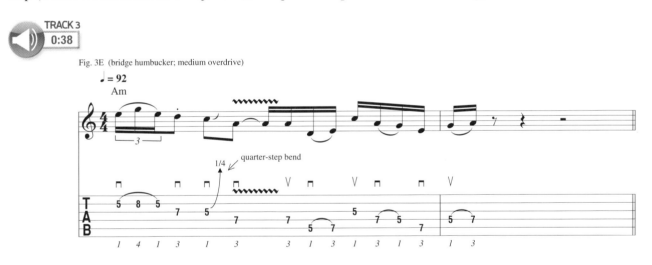

Fig. 3F is a funky lick fueled with a succession of palm-muted dead notes. (Refer to Figs. 3A and 3D.) This is a combination of two tricky techniques, so take it slow. Proper picking direction is the key factor here. Start with the picking directions in the example, but feel free to experiment with other combinations. Listen to the audio demonstration to make sure that you're getting the proper sound of the dead notes.

9

Connecting Pentatonic Patterns

Back-to-back legato ploys provide the rhythmic complexity of **Fig. 3G**. First up is a hammer/pull (refer to Fig. 3D) on the low-E string, followed by a "pull/hammer" on the adjacent A string. A pull/hammer is—you guessed it!— the opposite of a hammer/pull. Plant your ring (3rd) finger on the seventh fret of the A string, strike the string with the pick, and immediately pull off to the fifth fret (which your index finger should already be fretting), and then hammer on back to the seventh fret with your ring finger. Played in an eighth-note rhythm (eight eighth notes comprise one measure), the cycled three-note patterns provide an interesting "disturbance" in the 4/4-meter groove. This effective rhythmic technique will be explored further in upcoming solos.

TRACK 3
1:25

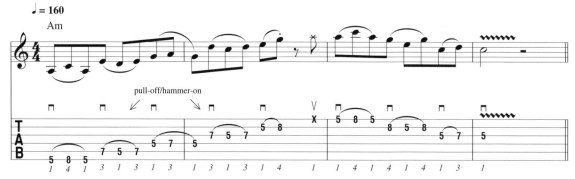

Sequencing Patterns and "Rollover" Techniques

The next few licks demonstrate handy phrase-building devices known as scale sequences. Loosely defined, a *scale sequence* is a specific pattern of scale tones that is repeated at various starting points within the same scale. **Fig. 4A** is an example of a "groups of 3" scale sequence cast in eighth-note triplet rhythms (three eighth notes in the space of two). A descending passage, it snakes its way down the scale in three-note increments: C–A–G, A–G–E, G–E–D, etc. Don't forget to "shuffle" the eighth notes at the end of the phrase (the first eighth note receives the value of two eighth notes from an eighth-note triplet). (Note: explaining all of the rhythms notated in the licks is beyond the scope of this "hands on" book. Just remember that you can always listen to the examples on the accompanying audio for clarification. For a complete breakdown of rhythmic notation, however, check out Chapter 2 of *Music Theory for Guitarists* [Hal Leonard].)

TRACK 4
0:00

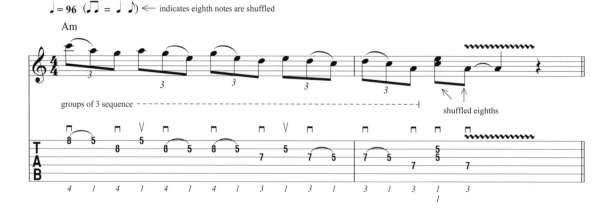

Fig. 4B provides another example of a "groups of 3" sequence. Notice how the strategic inclusion of the quarter-step bends (refer to Fig. 3E) helps break up the (potentially) predictable nature of the phrase. Led Zeppelin's Jimmy Page is a famous purveyor of the "groups of 3" sequence. The outro solo in "Good Times Bad Times" provides a fire-breathing example of the sequence in action.

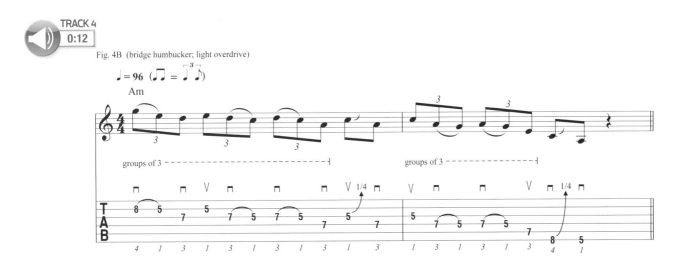

Fig. 4B (bridge humbucker; light overdrive)

Another popular scale sequence is the "groups of 4" sequence. Due to the rhythmic evenness of the pattern, the sequence works particularly well with eighth-note and 16th-note rhythm figures. **Fig. 4C** opens with an ascending "groups of 4" sequence, climbing the first four notes of Pattern 1 (A–C–D–E), with the second group starting on C, and then the third group starting on D. In measure 2, the pattern takes an interesting twist, descending in "groups of 4," but starting the next sequence one note *higher* in the scale! **Fig. 4D** begins with a descending "groups of 4" sequence in measure 1, then segues to a "groups of 3" sequence in measure 2.

Fig. 4C (bridge humbucker; medium overdrive)

Fig. 4D (neck & bridge humbucker; light overdrive)

Connecting Pentatonic Patterns

The sequenced lick in **Fig. 4E** is built for speed! Loosely based on a "groups of 5" scale sequence, it has more to do with the properties of the fretboard than the actual scale. Look at the tab staff and you'll understand the sequence right away. The pattern is established in the first five-note sequence: two pull-offs on adjacent strings are followed by a single note on the third string. The five-note pattern is repeated on the next string set, and then the next. The lick ends with a reversal of the pattern up the A, D, and G string set.

TRACK 4
0:52

Fig. 4E (bridge humbucker; medium overdrive)

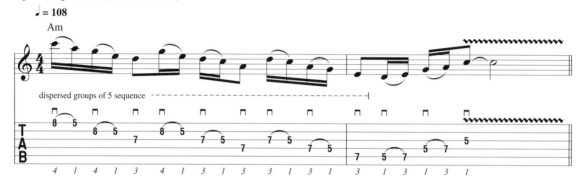

The next two examples require a tactic that this book will refer to as the "rollover" technique. **Fig. 4F** is a "note-jumping" sequence in which the phrase makes its way down the scale in two-note increments. Instead of descending the scale in traditional fashion (A–G–E–D–C–A, etc.), A "jumps" (or skips) over G to get to E, G leapfrogs E to get to D, and so on. Neal Schon's burning passage at the end of his solo in Journey's "Lights" provides a famous example of this sequence in action. Check out the fingering suggestions and you'll notice that the index (1st) and ring (3rd) fingers have to rollover to the next string when it's located on the same fret. This technique takes some practice, but the time invested is well worth the effort. Here's a tip (pun intended!) when moving from a higher string to an adjacent, lower string located at the same fret (as in the first two notes of the example): flatten out your index finger and fret the high-E string (in this case) with the fleshy part of your upper finger. Then, "roll" your finger over to fret the B string with the traditional fingertip area of the index finger. Once you've got this lick down, try out your freshly honed rollover technique on the 16th-note-based example in **Fig. 4G**.

TRACK 4
1:09

Fig. 4F (neck single coil; light overdrive)

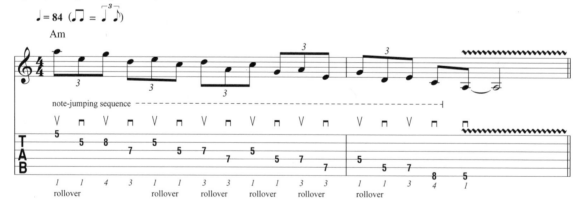

TRACK 4
1:29

Fig. 4G (bridge & middle single coil; medium overdrive)

Bends and Slides

The next three figures are examples of the string-bending techniques that will be used throughout the book. **Fig. 5A** opens with one of the most common bends in rock and blues: a "bend/release" on the G string. Make sure you bend the D note up a whole step to match the pitch E. And don't just bend with your ring (3rd) finger—use any available fingers to help with the bending chores; in this case, the middle (2nd) and index (1st) fingers are practical assistants. The second bend in the example is a "sustained bend." Grip the neck, dig in with your palm, and use the strength of all three of the digits behind your pinky to hold that bend. If you can, give the note a vibrato "wiggle" (release slightly and bend back to pitch several times) when you reach the pitch destination (A).

TRACK 5
0:00

Fig. 5A (neck single coil; medium overdrive)

Fig. 5B begins with a "choke bend," whereby you bend to pitch and immediately mute the string with your fretting hand before you release the bend. In this case, mute the G-string bend with the underside of your thumb as it passes over to pick the high-E string. For the grace-note choke bend, you can use the heel of the palm of your fret hand to mute the G string.

TRACK 5
0:09

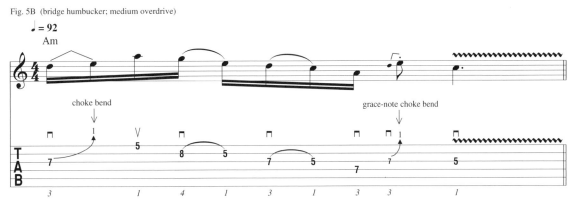
Fig. 5B (bridge humbucker; medium overdrive)

Fig. 5C incorporates three different grace-note bends. Make sure you bend to pitch very quickly for all three moves.

TRACK 5
0:23

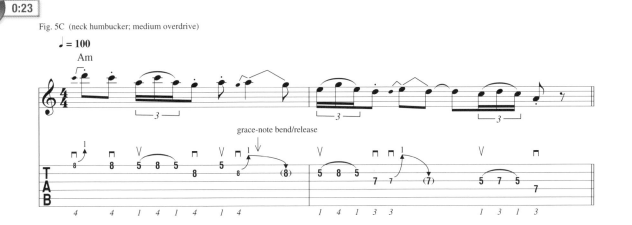
Fig. 5C (neck humbucker; medium overdrive)

Connecting Pentatonic Patterns

The next set of figures introduces the *slide*, or *legato slide* technique. A legato slide is performed by striking a note and then sliding the same fretting finger up or down to a second note without striking the string again. Slide techniques are some of the most important tools for connecting pentatonic patterns and will be used throughout this book, so take the time to work out these slippery Pattern 1 licks. They're all designed to strengthen the index finger. We'll get to the other digits very soon!

Fig. 5D features three identical slide maneuvers. Although they are performed on different strings, they all start from the fifth fret, slide up to the seventh, and return to the fifth—all with just one string attack. Remember to keep pressure on the fretting finger so the notes will sound nice and even. **Fig. 5E** is a similar lick but ends with a pair of pull-offs. **Fig. 5F** includes a "pull/slide," whereby the slide is preceded by a pull-off.

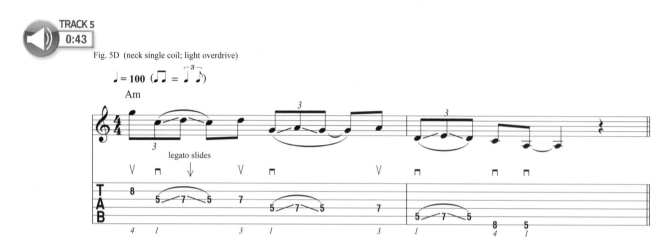

Fig. 5D (neck single coil; light overdrive)

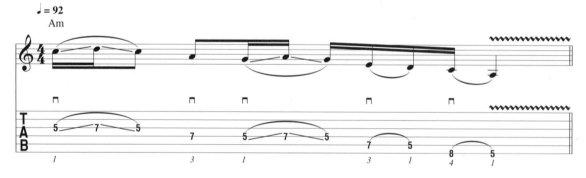

Fig. 5E (bridge humbucker; medium overdrive)

TRACK 5
1:14

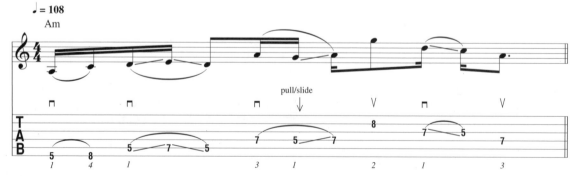

Fig. 5F (neck & middle single coil; medium overdrive)

Double Stops and String Skipping

A good way to fortify your pentatonic solos is to use *double stops*—two notes played simultaneously, on adjacent strings. Many rock and blues guitarists incorporate double stops into their playing, but the undisputed master is Jimi Hendrix ("The Wind Cries Mary," "Little Wing," etc.). **Fig. 6A** is reminiscent of Jimi's R&B (rhythm & blues) stylings. Note the use of grace-note hammer-ons for the C/A and G/E doubles stops. In both cases, use your index (1st) finger to barre across the strings at the fifth fret, hammering on to the seventh fret with your ring (3rd) finger. Use the same index-finger barre method to navigate the double-stop hammer-ons in **Fig. 6B** and **Fig. 6C**.

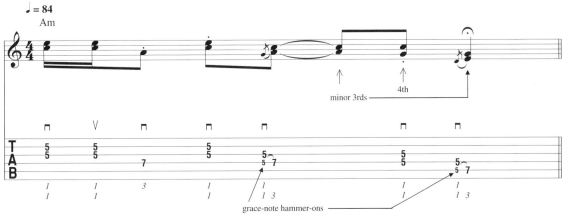

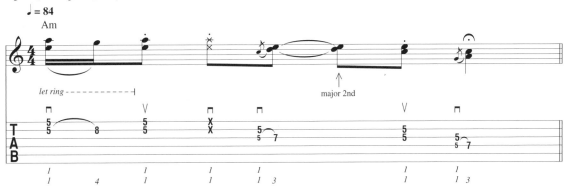

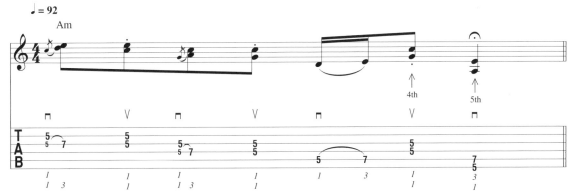

Quick Theory Tutorial #2

Another name for double stops is *harmonic intervals*, or just *intervals*. A wide array of harmonic intervals is within your grasp in Pattern 1. For instance, couple the notes at the fifth fret of the high-E and B strings and you have a 4th interval (2-1/2 steps). Intervals of a 4th are also available by pairing the same strings at the eighth fret, the G and D strings at the fifth or seventh fret, the D and A strings at the same frets, and the A and low-E string at the fifth fret. Pair the seventh fret of the G string and the eighth fret of the B string for another 4th interval.

Other useful sets of intervals include minor 3rds (1-1/2 steps), major 3rds (two whole steps), and major 2nds (one whole step). Here are some combinations:

Minor 3rd: fifth-fret G string/seventh-fret D string, fifth-fret D string/seventh-fret A string

Major 3rd: fifth-fret B string/fifth-fret G string, seventh-fret A string/eighth-fret low-E string

Major 2nd: fifth-fret high-E string/eighth-fret B string, fifth-fret B string/seventh-fret G string

Fig. 6D is an ambitious example that links double stops with hammer/pulls and slides. Take it slowly, working out the fingering and picking suggestions. Refer to the audio demonstration for aural clarification.

TRACK 6
0:36

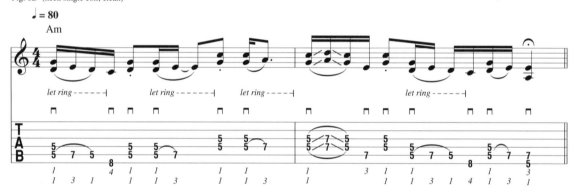

Fig. 6D (neck single coil; clean)

String skipping (or "string jumping") is an effective device for adding pizzazz to your solos. Essentially, string skipping is when you pass over one or more strings to play the next note on a non-adjacent string. (Listen to Eric Johnson's "Cliffs of Dover" to hear a tour de force of string-skipping tactics.) **Fig. 6E** is a riff-like example that uses string skipping to climb Pattern 1 in "jumpy" increments. The picking directions are crafted so that you're plucking downward on the lower string before the string skip. This helps provide momentum to jump over the "in between" string while positioning your hand to pluck upward on the higher string. Some guitarists refer to this as "outside picking"—that is, picking on the "outsides" of the string sets, be they adjacent strings or non-adjacent. Outside picking is used exclusively in the rapid-fire, string-skipping example in **Fig. 6F**.

TRACK 6
1:02

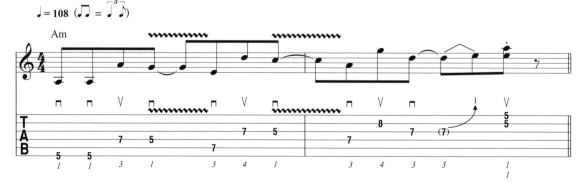

Fig. 6E (bridge single coil; medium/heavy overdrive)

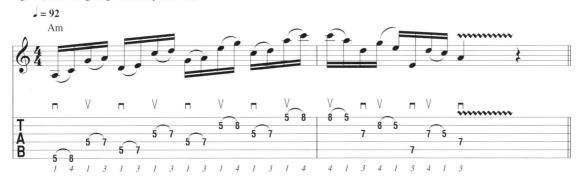

Fig. 6F (neck & bridge single coil; heavy overdrive)

Extension Boxes

Many pentatonic masters squeeze extra mileage out of Pattern 1 with the help of two "extension boxes." **Fig. 7A** illustrates where these boxes are located and how they correspond to Pattern 1. The "lower extension box" is a box of notes (G–A–C–D) located at the third and fifth frets of the low-E and A strings. In actuality, only one note is being added here: G (third fret of the low-E string). The A and D notes are part of Pattern 1, and the C note (third fret of the A string) is the same note as the one at the eighth fret of the low-E string. Re-positioning the C and adding the G note fortifies Pattern 1, increasing its lick-making potential, as we'll see in a moment. First, let's look at the upper extension box.

The upper extension box contains five notes (E–G–A–C–D) and is located on the G, B, and high-E string set. It actually looks a bit more like an upside-down pentagon than a box, but it's a box shape nonetheless. As a matter of fact, many players refer to it as the "Albert King box," as it's a great pattern for emulating that legendary player's famous blues licks. Again, only one note is being added here: D (10th fret of the high-E string). The E and A notes are simply moved from their fifth-fret positions, and the G and C notes are the "linking notes" to Pattern 1.

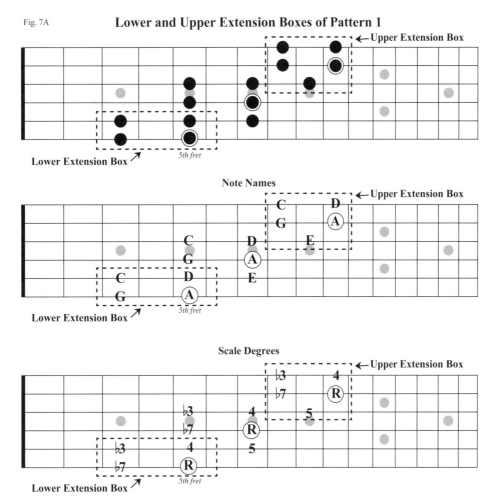

Fig. 7A   **Lower and Upper Extension Boxes of Pattern 1**

17

Connecting Pentatonic Patterns

Fig. 7B offers fingering suggestions for connecting the two extension boxes to Pattern 1. Start in the lower extension box with your index (1st) finger on G. When you reach the top of the box with your ring (3rd) finger on D, use a "shift slide" to arrive at the seventh-fret E. A *shift slide* is just like a legato slide, except the second note is struck. (You could also use a legato slide, if you prefer.) Now you're connected to Pattern 1. From here, you're in familiar territory until you reach D at the seventh fret of the G string, where you'll again use a shift slide to connect with the upper extension box. Some players like to use their middle (2nd) finger for the shift, while others favor the ring (3rd) finger. Experiment to determine which approach works best for you. Once you arrive in the upper extension box, you still have multiple fingering options. Although there are many combinations, the example depicts two useable fingerings. **Fig. 7C** offers fingering suggestions for descending from the upper extension box, through the middle of Pattern 1, and into the lower extension box. Here, descending shift slides are used to make the connections.

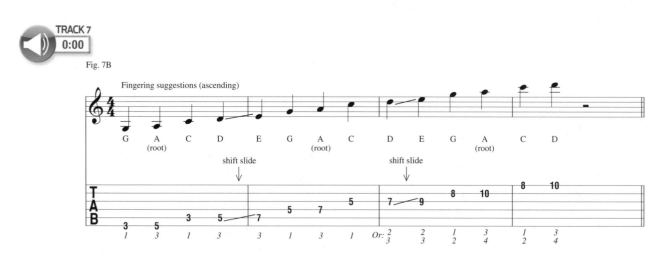

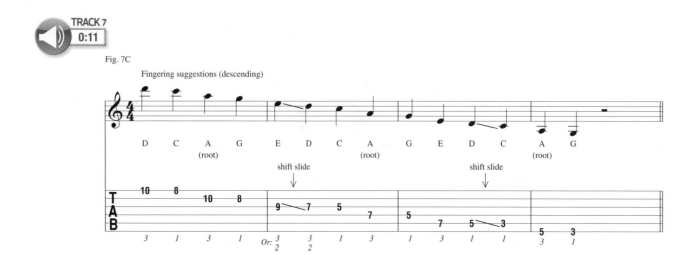

18

Lower Extension Box Examples

Fig. 8A is a growling lick that starts in the lower extension box and uses a legato slide to connect with Pattern 1. Liberal use of downpicking gives the lick a heavy attitude. **Fig. 8B** starts in Pattern 1 and segues to the lower extension box with the help of a legato slide/pull-off maneuver. Palm muting gives the lick its "thudding" character, while a pinch harmonic puts a nasty sparkle on the last note. To produce the pinch harmonic, pick down hard on the string while you simultaneously let the side of your pick-hand thumb brush the string as it passes over. Zakk Wylde (Ozzy Ozbourne, Black Label Society) and Billy Gibbons (ZZ Top) are masters of pinch-harmonic technique. **Fig. 8C** makes liberal use of legato maneuvers throughout. Low and funky, it's reminiscent of something Aerosmith's Joe Perry might play.

TRACK 8 0:00

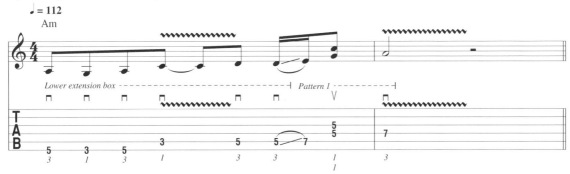

Fig. 8A (bridge humbucker; medium/heavy overdrive)

TRACK 8 0:08

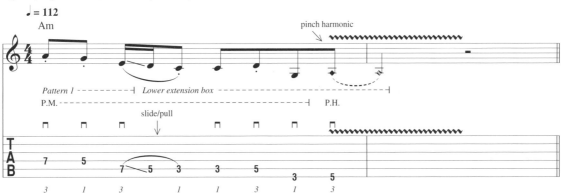

Fig. 8B (bridge humbucker; medium/heavy overdrive)

TRACK 8 0:17

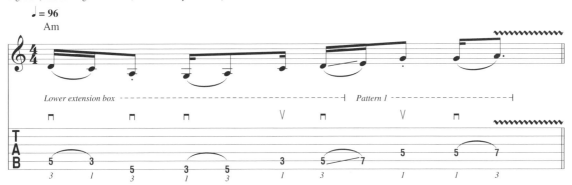

Fig. 8C (neck & bridge humbucker; medium/heavy overdrive)

Connecting Pentatonic Patterns

The bluesy lick in **Fig. 8D** uses a "groups of 3" sequence (see Figs. 4A–B) to descend from Pattern 1 to the lower extension box. The funk-rock example in **Fig. 8E** starts in the lower extension box and culminates with a set of double stops (see Figs. 6A–D). The note in parentheses is a "sympathetic" note that is unintentionally sounded by the fretting fingers. It actually sounds good, so we'll consider it a happy accident!

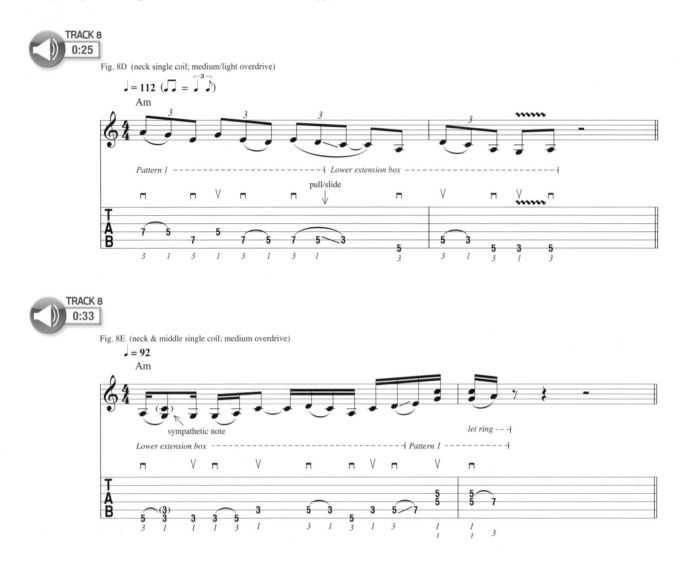

TRACK 8 0:25

Fig. 8D (neck single coil; medium/light overdrive)

TRACK 8 0:33

Fig. 8E (neck & middle single coil; medium overdrive)

Fig. 8F opens with a *melodic motif*, a melodic or rhythmic pattern that is repeated or developed with variations, which is "answered" by a tricky lick in the lower extension box that involves a rollover maneuver (see Fig. 4F).

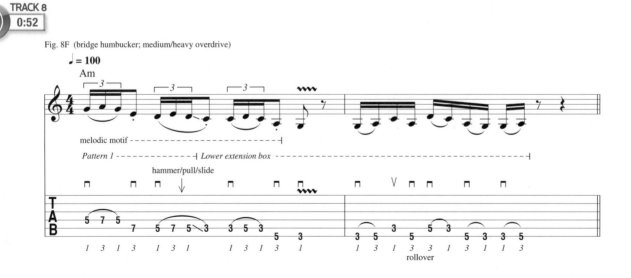

TRACK 8 0:52

Fig. 8F (bridge humbucker; medium/heavy overdrive)

Upper Extension Box Examples

Fig. 9A is a stock blues-rock phrase that starts on the "middle" root (remember: there are three of them) of Pattern 1 and moves up into the upper extension box. If you have trouble reaching up with your middle (2nd) finger to make the shift, here's a tip: tilt your fretting hand a bit by dropping the pinky side of your wrist toward the floor. This should make the reach much more comfortable.

TRACK 9
0:00

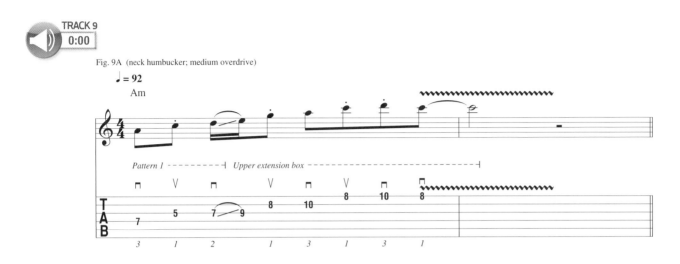

Fig. 9A (neck humbucker; medium overdrive)

Fig. 9B descends from the upper extension box into the midpoint of Pattern 1. A grace-note slide maneuver links the two boxes. Using the ring (3rd) finger for the shift is a bit tricky, but it positions your fret hand perfectly for the remainder of the phrase. Incidentally, the fifth-fret G-string microtone bend in parentheses is notation for a "delayed bend," whereby the fretted note is sustained for a designated amount of time before it's bent.

TRACK 9
0:10

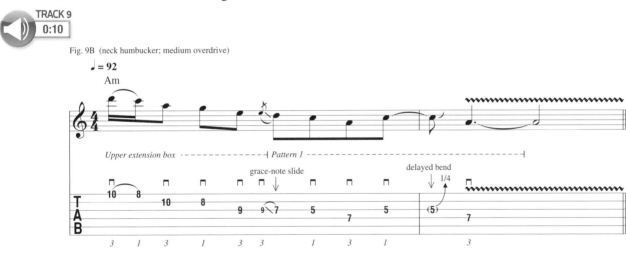

Fig. 9B (neck humbucker; medium overdrive)

The bluesy example in **Fig. 9C** opens with a melodic motif (see Fig. 8F) and closes with a string-jumping lick (see Figs. 6E–F). Outside picking (also refer to Figs. 6E–F) is employed throughout.

TRACK 9
0:21

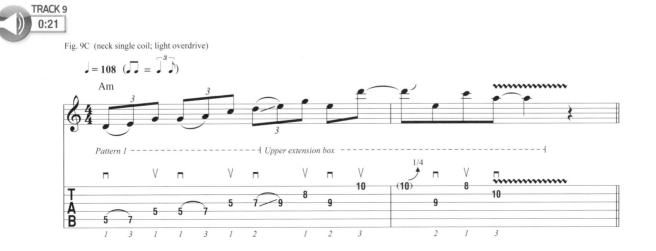

Fig. 9C (neck single coil; light overdrive)

Connecting Pentatonic Patterns

Fig. 9D is essentially a revved-up combination of Figs. 9A–B. Notice that this time the middle (2nd) finger is used for the shift back into Pattern 1. This is purely a matter of preference here, so feel free to use your ring (3rd) finger if you want.

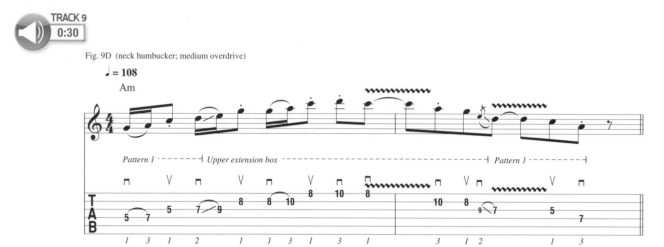

Fig. 9E is a double-stop phrase (see Figs. 6A–D) designed to emulate the sound of a blues harp (i.e., harmonica). Be sure to let the *dyads* (another name for double stops) ring together.

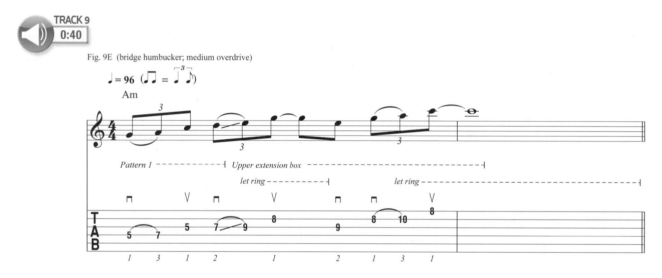

Fig. 9F climbs the neck from the lower extension box, through the middle of Pattern 1, and all the way to the top of the upper extension box! Look carefully and you'll see that the first three notes establish a pattern that continues through the entire lick: two notes on a lower string followed by one note on the adjacent, higher string. A hammer-on services the first trio of notes while a slide maneuver sends the next set of notes up the neck. **Fig. 9G** takes the opposite approach, descending from the upper extension box to the lower box. A similar three-note pattern is used in this lick, only in reverse.

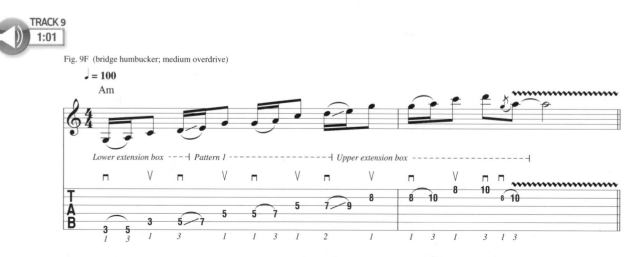

Fig. 9G (bridge humbucker; medium overdrive)

Combining All Regions of Pattern 1 with the Extension Boxes

Now that we have a handle on connecting the lower and upper extension boxes to the midsection of Pattern 1, it's time to incorporate them with the entire region of Pattern 1. Take a look at **Fig. 10A**. Pattern 1 is outlined by a solid black-line border, while the extension boxes are enclosed by dashed lines. The previous examples made heavy use of the "linking notes," but avoided the "doubled notes." Linking notes are the ones that share the borders of each box. (Refer to the upper neck diagram in Fig. 10A.) Doubled notes are notes of the same register that appear in different areas along the fretboard. (Refer to the lower neck diagram in Fig. 10A.) Understanding this is crucial, so let's take a look at some examples to clarify the concept.

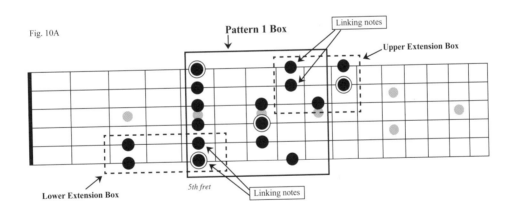

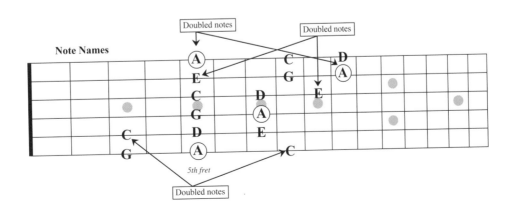

Connecting Pentatonic Patterns

Combination Licks

Fig. 10B incorporates the entire lower half of Pattern 1, dropping down to the lower extension box at the last moment. The lick just wouldn't be the same if the C note were played in the lower extension box. **Fig. 10C** starts in the lower extension box, using an interesting index-finger slide to segue into the lower portion of Pattern 1. **Fig. 10D** is a cool lick that would be perfect for a rock shuffle, such as ZZ Top's "Tush." Notice that the low C note is played first in Pattern 1, and then in the lower extension box.

Fig. 10B (bridge humbucker; medium/light overdrive)

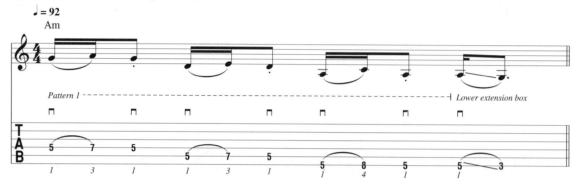

Fig. 10C (bridge humbucker; medium overdrive)

Fig. 10D (bridge humbucker; medium overdrive)

Fig. 10E calls to mind Eric Clapton's phrasing in Cream's "Crossroads." Notice that the high root (A) is played first in Pattern 1, and then again in the upper extension box. **Fig. 10F** is a bluesy lick that hosts a sneaky, ring (3rd) finger slide from the upper extension box to the top of Pattern 1. The essence of Clapton is present again in **Fig. 10G**. Picking direction is key to successfully navigating this challenging lick.

TRACK 10 0:37

Fig. 10E (neck & bridge humbucker; medium overdrive)

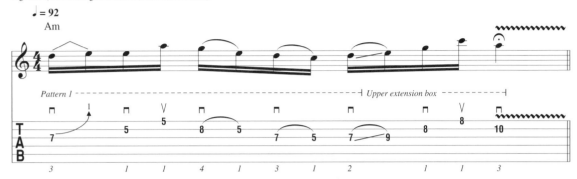

TRACK 10 0:54

Fig. 10F (neck single coil; light overdrive)

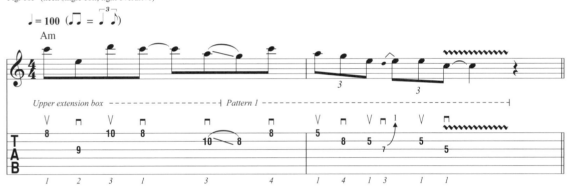

TRACK 10 1:05

Fig. 10G (neck & middle single coil; medium overdrive)

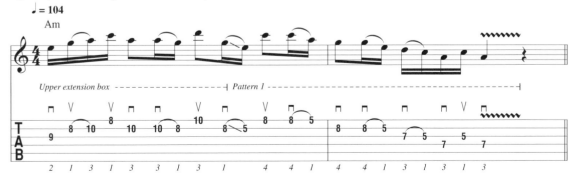

Connecting Pentatonic Patterns

Fig. 10H is a shuffle lick that slithers back and forth between the top regions of Pattern 1 and the upper extension box. **Fig. 10I** covers the same territory, but with a different feel and an interesting shift change via an index-finger slide down the high-E string.

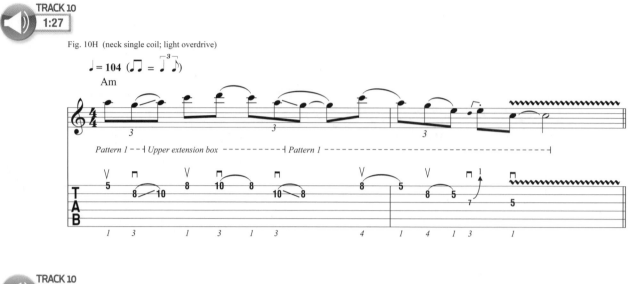

Fig. 10H (neck single coil; light overdrive)

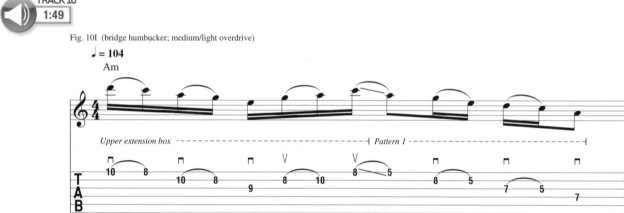

Fig. 10I (bridge humbucker; medium/light overdrive)

Fig. 10J is a sweet R&B double-stop phrase à la Jimi Hendrix and Steve Cropper (Otis Redding, Booker T. and the MGs). Take your time with this one, as it's a deceptively difficult passage. There's no room for shift slides—you actually have to "bounce" from dyad to dyad.

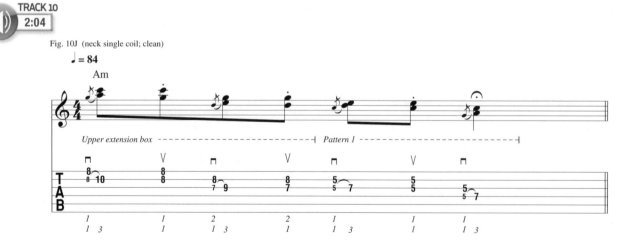

Fig. 10J (neck single coil; clean)

Fig. 10K is an example of sliding 4th intervals (see Quick Tutorial #2), a trademark of jazz-rock guitarist Larry Carlton. Look no further than his fills in Joni Mitchell's "Help Me." Nile Rodger's intro to David Bowie's "China Girl" is exclusively comprised of 4th intervals.

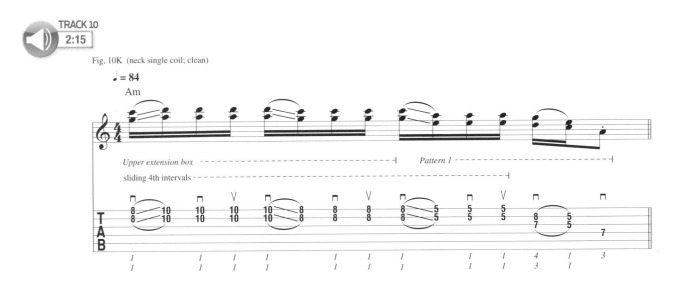

Solo 1A

Style: Melodic Hard Rock
Patterns: Pattern 1 with Upper and Lower Extension Boxes
Skill Level: Beginner/Intermediate

Fig. 11 is the complete transcription for the lead guitar in "Solo 1A." All of the licks and phrases are drawn from Pattern 1 of the A minor pentatonic scale and its lower and upper extension boxes. The solo is 32 measures in length and is backed by an entire rhythm section (drums, bass, and rhythm guitars). The style is melodic hard rock and the tempo is a moderate 104 beats per minute (bpm). The key is A minor. The form is based on an Am–F–Am (i–♭VI–i) chord sequence that is established in the first eight measures. This same eight-bar section is repeated in measures 9–16. Measures 17–24 serve as a "bridge" section, where C and G chords enter the mix. The final eight measures are the "outro" section, which is a slight variation of the opening section. (The chord frames at the top of the transcription offer some basic "grips" of the chords mentioned.)

Measures 1–8:
The solo opens in Pattern 1 with a simple phrase embellished with a pair of grace-note hammer-ons (see Fig. 6A). This leads to a bending phrase similar to the one explained in Fig. 5B, except this one ends with a bend/release/pull maneuver (immediately pull-off to a lower note after releasing the bend). Notice that this lick doesn't start on the downbeat of the measure; it's delayed by an eighth rest, coming in on the "and" of beat 1 (the upbeat). Rhythmic surprises such as this are a good way to avoid monotony and predictability in your solos. This lick spills into a two-bar phrase (measures 3–4) that employs a legato slide to slip down into the lower extension box (refer to Fig. 8B). The next two licks are variations of the simple melody established in measure 1. The first variation (measure 5) starts an octave lower, in the lower extension box, spilling into the second variation (measure 6), which is played in the same area as the introduction phrase (Pattern 1). (You can refer to Figs. 8A–C if you need help with the legato maneuvers.) This leads to the section closer: a straightforward blues-rock phrase in the upper extension box similar to the one explained in Fig. 9A.

Measures 9–16:

Measures 9–12 house an extended phrase that combines the moves discussed in Figs. 9F–G. This gradually descending passage travels all the way from the top of the upper extension box, through the midpoint of Pattern 1, and down into the lower extension box. Beat 4 of measure 12 begins a rhythmic motif that is carried through measures 13 and 14. Similar to the melodic motif defined in Fig. 8F, a *rhythmic motif* is a specific rhythmic pattern that is repeated, but with less emphasis on the melodic structure. Comprised of two 16th notes and the length of a quarter note, the motif climbs its way back up the neck in three-note increments: A–G–A, C–D–C, D–E–G, G–A–C. A crafty little passage, it exploits a lot of the legato techniques discussed in this chapter. The final lick of the section (measures 15–16) begins with a super-legato maneuver that we haven't discussed yet. Based on the hammer-on/pull-off technique explained in Fig. 3D, it's basically the same move performed twice in a row. We'll call it a "double hammer/pull." (The same technique, sped up and cycled, is called a *trill*.) This is immediately followed by a speedy little phrase that is based on the same principals as the five-note sequence lick explained in Fig. 4E.

Measures 17–24:

The next section begins with an "anticipated phrase" (a phrase that arrives early or starts in the previous measure) that contains a C/G "4ths dyad." A 4ths dyad is a double stop constructed from the interval of a perfect 4th. (Refer to Quick Theory Tutorial #2.) This is followed by a couple of legato moves that contain delayed resolution. In other words, notes are sustained before they result in a pull-off, hammer-on, or slide. In the first one, the D note is held before it's pulled off to C (between measures 17 and 18); in the second one, E is held before it slides down to D (measure 18). The rhythms are a bit tricky in measures 19–22, so go slowly, and check your progress with the audio demonstration. Measure 23 is the official closing lick for the section. Another motif, it's both rhythmic and melodic in structure. The rhythm pattern is a strict three 16ths plus a dotted 8th, and the melody stays consistent with a step-by-step, sequenced scale descent.

Measures 25–32:

The outro section begins with another early entry (anticipated) phrase. This one also starts on the "and of 3" of the previous measure. Similar in structure to the neck-climbing lick in Fig. 9F, it's an extended phrase (measures 24–28) that ascends incrementally from the third fret of the low-E string, all the way to the 10th fret of the high E, where it backs off to resolve on the upper root (A) at the 10th fret of the B string. In measure 28, gravity takes effect and the solo goes out with a series of licks that make their way down the upper extension box, through the middle of Pattern 1, and down into the lower extension box. Be careful with those bends in measure 29. Although similar in melody, they're two different techniques entirely. One is a sustained bend with vibrato (see Fig. 5A), while the other is a choke bend (refer to Fig. 5B).

Tone Tips

Guitar: solidbody electric

Pickup Selection: bridge

Pickup Type: humbucker

Gain: 8 (pre-amp volume: 1–3 = clean; 4–7 = medium overdrive; 8–10 = heavy overdrive)

EQ: Bass/Middle/Treble: 5/8/3

Effects: moderate reverb (large hall), moderate delay with long slap (approx. 580ms)

Fig. 11 "Solo 1A"

Connecting Pentatonic Patterns

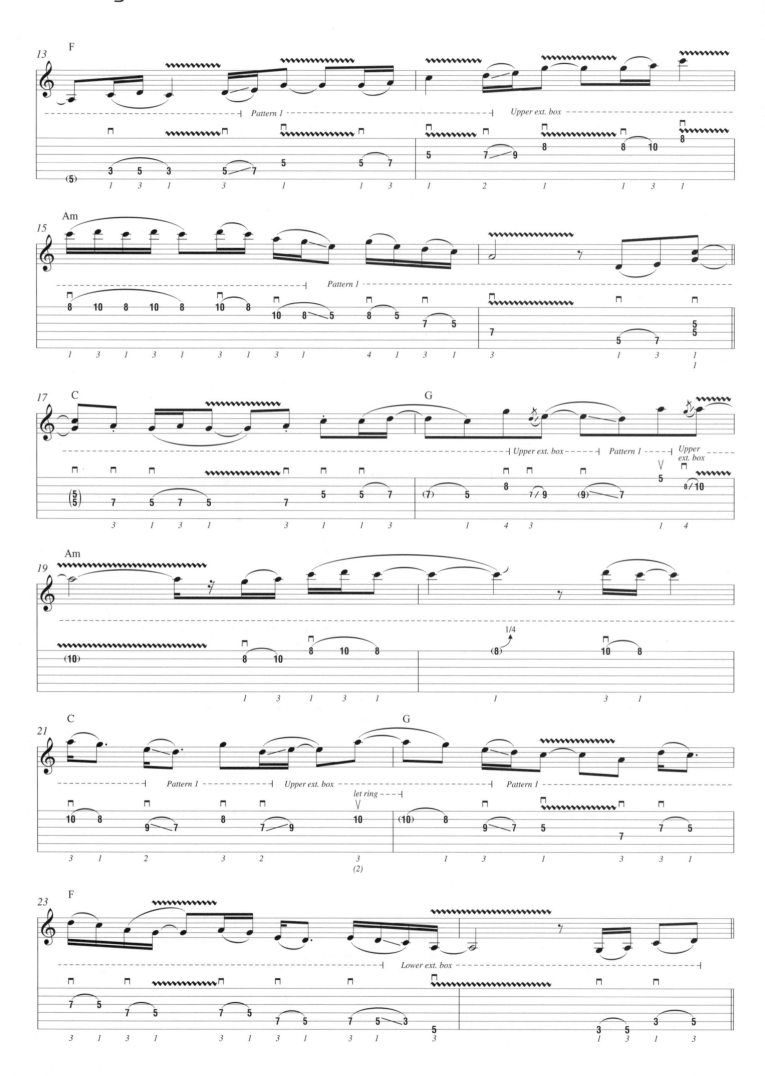

Solo 1B

Style: Melodic Hard Rock
Patterns: Pattern 1 with Upper and Lower Extension Boxes
Skill Level: Intermediate/Advanced

Solo 1B **[Fig. 12]** is performed over the exact same chord progression and rhythm track as Solo 1A. Although performed at the same tempo, Solo 1B is designed to be a technically advanced version of Solo 1A.

Measures 1–8:

The solo opens with a tricky hammer/pull and a jump to the D string. Keep your fretting fingers arched—don't flatten them out across the fretboard. And be careful with the segue from measure 2 to measure 3; it contains a rather "backwards" cascade down Pattern 1, where a series of hammer-ons are launched from the fifth fret to the higher notes in the pattern. In measure 4, make sure to let the D note ring when you slide the subsequent low G up to A. The result should be a sustained A5 (A–E) power chord. Measures 5 and 6 juggle legato licks between Pattern

1 and the lower extension box. Remember, the picking directions are suggestions, so feel free to craft them to your personal taste. Measures 7 and 8 contain some slippery moves between the upper extension box and Pattern 1. Use an index-finger rollover (see Fig. 4F) to grab the sequential seventh-fret notes in measure 7.

Measures 9–16:

Take a deep breath because the action is pretty much non-stop in measures 9–16. Taking it one bar at a time, measure 9 opens with a "pedal-tone" lick (E is the pedal tone) in the upper extension box. (This lick incorporates the string-skipping tactics discussed in Figs. 6E–F.) Next, we have a set of Dickey Betts-style (Allman Brothers) double-slide moves that use tactics discussed in Figs. 5D–F, then comes a speedy legato lick that starts on the seventh fret of the G string and falls all the way down Pattern 1 (end of measure 10, into measure 11). Don't be afraid of this lick—it's actually easier than it looks or sounds! The lick that follows is yet another variation of the basic "neck climber" from Fig. 9F. The double-stop passage in measure 13 is based on the sliding-4ths example in Fig. 10K. Approach it as if you were strumming chords. Next is a short Hendrix-style passage (refer to Figs. 6A–D), followed by another rapid set of pull-offs like the ones in measure 11, and the section goes out with a pull-off driven descent into the lower extension box (measures 15–16). Take a lot of time with that five-note, pull/slide/hammer/pull, super-legato lick. It's a great move for zipping up-and-down a single string. For examples, check out "May This Be Love" by Jimi Hendrix or Eric Clapton's solo in Cream's "I'm So Glad."

Measures 17–24:

Double stops quickly become the theme of this section. As you piece them together, strive for the finesse of the Hendrix-style examples explained in Figs. 6A–D, but with the spirited, reckless abandon of a soloist like Neil Young! The distorted tone really brings out the harmonics, making them sound thicker than they do with a clean tone. But you need to be extra careful so as to mute the surrounding strings with any available fretting finger. Otherwise, the result could be a muddy mess.

Measures 25–32:

In the closing section, further double-stop adventures ensue, commingling with legato lines similar to the ones used in Solo 1A. Highlights include the ringing dyads in measure 25 (discussed in Fig. 9E) and the "copycat" phrases in measures 29 and 30. And don't overlook the subtle microtone bend (see Fig. 3E) applied to the fifth-fret double stop at the end of measure 26. This move hearkens back to Chuck Berry ("Johnny B. Goode"), one of the forefathers of rock lead guitar.

Tone Tips

Guitar: solidbody electric

Pickup Selection: bridge

Pickup Type: humbucker

Gain: 8

EQ: Bass/Middle/Treble: 5/8/3

Effects: moderate reverb (large hall), moderate delay with long slap (approx. 580ms)

🔊 TRACK 12

Fig. 12 "Solo 1B"

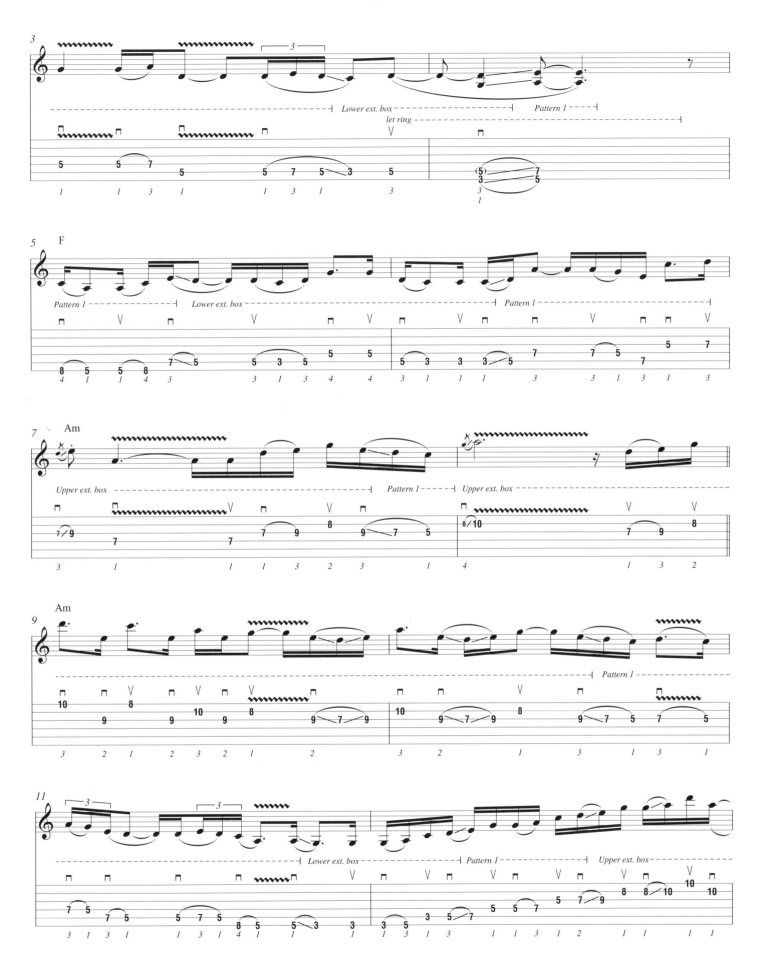

Connecting Pentatonic Patterns

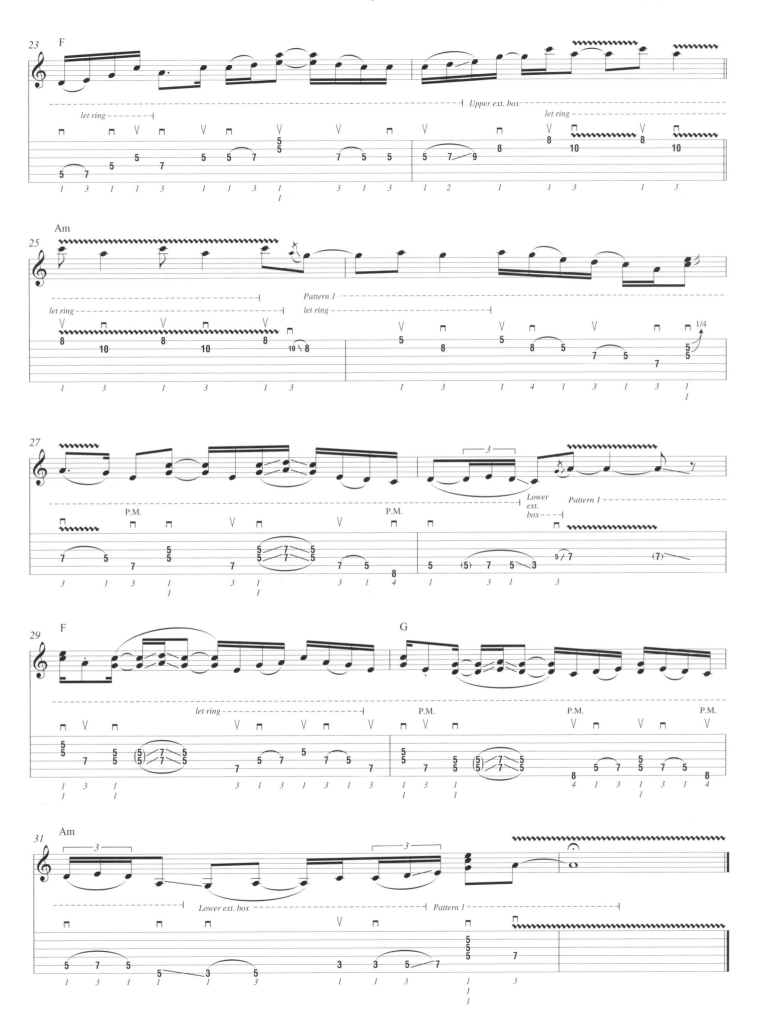

CHAPTER 2

PATTERN 2:
Connecting Patterns 1 and 2

This chapter introduces Pattern 2 of the minor pentatonic scale and methods for connecting it with Pattern 1.

Pattern 2 of the A Minor Pentatonic Scale

Fig. 13A shows Pattern 2 of the A minor pentatonic scale. The top neck diagram simply illustrates the location of the notes, while the diagram below it shows the note names. The third neck diagram depicts the scale degrees. Notice that the lowest root of this pattern is located on the seventh fret of the D string. From there, it goes up the scale to hit the octave root on the 10th fret of the B string, and then two notes further, C and D. The positioning of the top five notes (E–G–A–C–D) probably looks familiar. That's because they're from the upper extension box of Pattern 1 (see Fig. 7A). The notes on the A and low-E strings are called the "notes below the root," and they descend down the scale to the lowest note in the pattern, C, or the ♭3rd of the scale.

Fig. 13A

Pattern 2

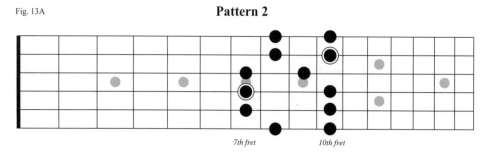

Note Names

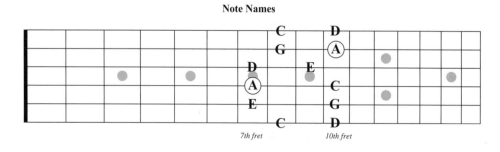

Scale Degrees

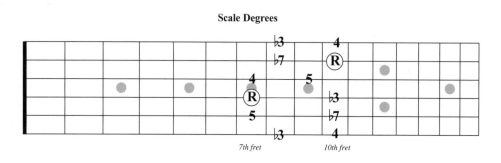

Fig. 13B shows two slightly different sets of fret-hand fingering suggestions. Depending on the lick, one usually works better than the other. Practice playing up and down the scale pattern, first with one fingering, then the other. You'll notice that the example doesn't start on the lowest note of the pattern; instead, it starts on the lowest *root* (A), goes up the scale to the highest note in the pattern (D), comes back down to the lowest note (C), and then travels up to end on the original starting point. Get used to practicing Pattern 2 in this fashion at first. That way, you're training your ear to retain the sound of the A minor pentatonic scale while you're "burning in" your muscle memory of the pattern.

TRACK 13

Fig. 13B

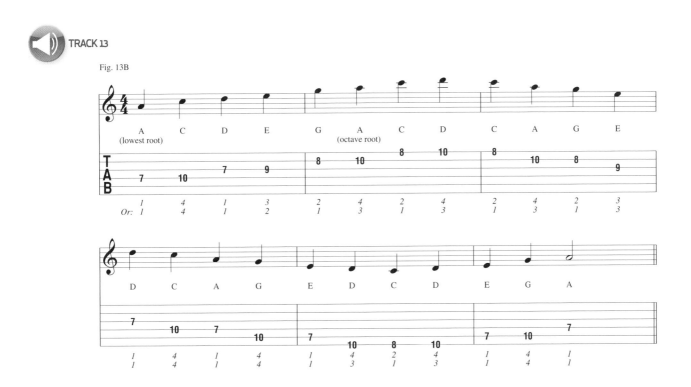

Pattern 2 Licks

Fig. 14A is a simple blues-shuffle lick (see Fig. 4A) that sounds just as good over an A7 chord (A–C♯–E–G) as it does for an Am (A–C–E) or Am7 (A–C–E–G). (Refer to Quick Theory Tutorial #3.) The lick goes right up the scale from the root (A) to the 5th (E), and with a grace-note slide, caps off in the upper portion of the pattern. Note the quarter-step bend on the ♭3rd (C). This gives the lick an edgy sound. The problem is that the bend needs to be performed with the index finger. This can be difficult because the other fingers can't join in to help with the "lifting" chores (see Fig. 5A). When dealing with index-finger bends, wrap your thumb around the top of the fretboard and squeeze down while you bend your index finger up to meet it. **Fig. 14B** travels the same fretboard terrain as the previous lick, but in descending fashion. Notice that the ♭3rd (C) in this lick also gets the quarter-step "nudge." **Fig. 14C** is another shuffle lick, but in the lower register of Pattern 2. And, here again, the ♭3rd is bent slightly, this time on the low-E string.

TRACK 14
0:00

Fig. 14A (neck single coil; light overdrive)

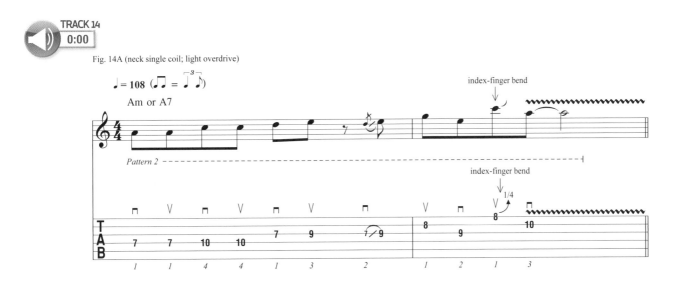

Connecting Pentatonic Patterns

TRACK 14
0:11

Fig. 14B (neck single coil/light overdrive)

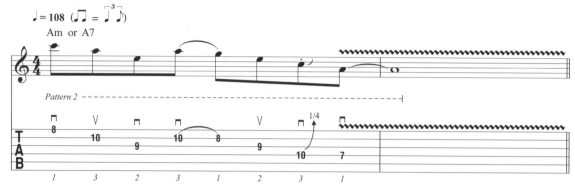

TRACK 14
0:21

Fig. 14C (neck single coil/light overdrive)

The 10th-fret bend in **Fig. 14D** squeezes an extra note out of Pattern 2 without leaving its boundaries. This is a classic example of the "Albert King box" in action (see Fig. 7A). **Fig. 14E** is a macho Stevie Ray Vaughan-style lick similar to the ones he played in songs like "Crossfire." Be careful on this one, as it requires brute strength and determination. Bend the high-E string with the ring (3rd) finger and let it catch, or "snag," the B string during the bend. (Make sure your ring finger is fretting the B string.) This results in a double-stop bend, whereby both notes are bent up in pitch simultaneously. Depending on the positioning of the finger, the results can vary. In this example, the results are an E/B dyad in the first bend and an E/C dyad in the second.

Quick Theory Tutorial #3

As previously discussed, the A minor pentatonic scale is a good source for soloing over Am (A–C–E) chords, as well as progressions that use chords from the A minor scale, like the ones in Solo 1A and 1B. However, blues guitarists also use the A minor pentatonic scale to solo over A7 (A–C♯–E–G) chords. Theoretically, the ♭3rd (C) of the scale clashes with the A7 (because the chord contains a C♯), but blues and blues-rock players enjoy the tension created from the (arguably) dissonant "rub." Blues music, in general, is full of tension notes and "notes between the notes," such as the quarter-step bends in some of the previous examples.

TRACK 14
0:32

Fig. 14D (neck single coil; light overdrive)

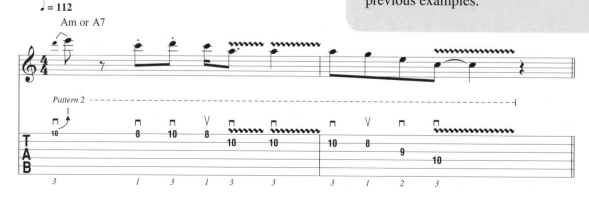

TRACK 14
0:41

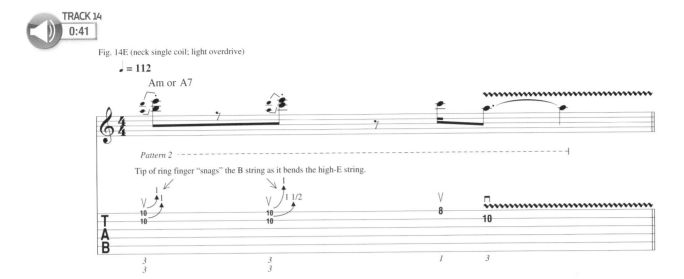

Fig. 14E (neck single coil; light overdrive)

Tip of ring finger "snags" the B string as it bends the high-E string.

Fig. 14F is another example of getting your money's worth out of the "Albert King box." This one begins with a *pre-bend*, whereby the string is already bent to pitch with the fretting finger before you strike the string with the pick. The "bonus" note is the step-and-a-half bend from the 10th fret of the B string. Stevie Ray Vaughan and David Gilmour (Pink Floyd) are well-known for using "wide bends" such as these.

TRACK 14
0:55

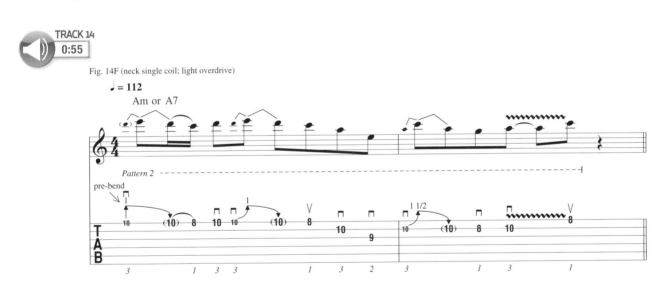

Fig. 14F (neck single coil; light overdrive)

Fig. 14G is in the double-stop style of Jimi Hendrix ("Little Wing," "The Wind Cries Mary"). This one starts with *pickup notes*. Pickup notes are notes that start before the downbeat of beat 1 of the first measure of the lick (or song), similar to the anticipated phrasing discussed in Solo 1A. The first note attack in this lick is on the last 16th note of beat 3. Here's a way to count yourself in: "*one*-ee-and-uh, *two*-ee-and-uh, *three*-ee-and…" The "uh" that's left out of the count on beat 3 is where you would enter with the first note, E.

TRACK 14
1:04

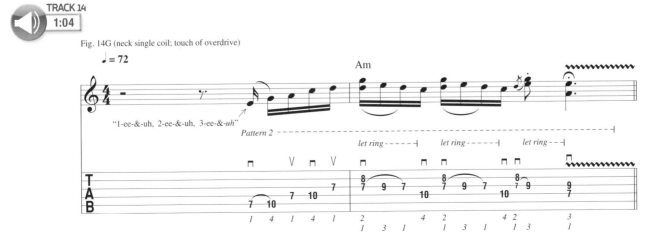

Fig. 14G (neck single coil; touch of overdrive)

Fig. 14H is a funky phrase in the style of John Frusciante (Red Hot Chili Peppers). It's played in the lower half of Pattern 2 and includes a lot of muted dead notes on adjacent strings (see Fig. 3A). These particular dead notes require muting the adjacent string (or strings) with the bottom of your fretting finger while using a heavy picking attack to simultaneously strike the fretted string and muted strings.

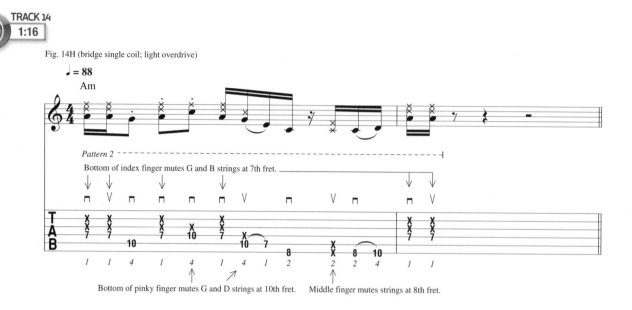

Fig. 14H (bridge single coil; light overdrive)

Connecting Patterns 1 and 2

The top neck diagram in **Fig. 15A** illustrates how Patterns 1 and 2 of the A minor pentatonic scale connect on the fretboard. The dashed lines outline Pattern 1, while the solid lines outline Pattern 2. Notice how they sort of "snap" together like pieces in a jigsaw puzzle. Be aware that the lowest note (A) in Pattern 1 is located at the fifth fret, while the lowest note (C) in Pattern 2 is at the eighth fret. The notes at the seventh and eighth frets are common to both patterns and are referred to as "linking notes." The second neck diagram illustrates these linking notes, boxing them in with a dashed-line border.

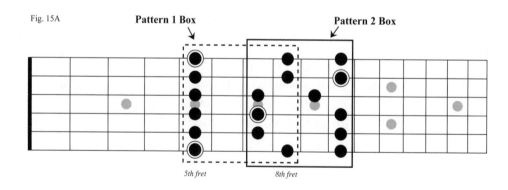

Fig. 15A

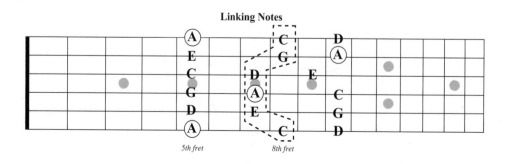

Lick Examples That Combine Patterns 1 and 2

Fig. 15B is an *arpeggiated* lick (notes of a chord played individually) that starts in Pattern 1 and slides up to Pattern 2 via the D-string linking note (A). Incidentally, the arpeggio is Am7 (A–C–E–G) and is played in two octaves.

TRACK 15
0:00

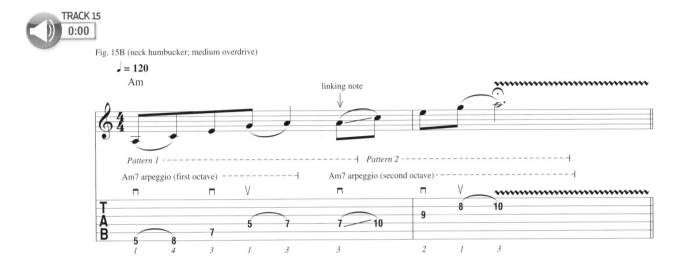

Fig. 15B (neck humbucker; medium overdrive)

Fig. 15C uses the same linking note, but in a descending lick reminiscent of Joe Walsh (James Gang, Eagles). A funky lick, it comes right down the scale from the octave root of Pattern 2, connecting to Pattern 1 with a slide from the linking note (A) on the D string. And speaking of the Eagles… here's a lick [**Fig. 15D**] in the style of Don Felder. Similar to his solo break in "Hotel California," it features a wide bend (see Fig. 14F) in Pattern 2 and a cool hammer/pull/slide segue down to Pattern 1.

TRACK 15
0:11

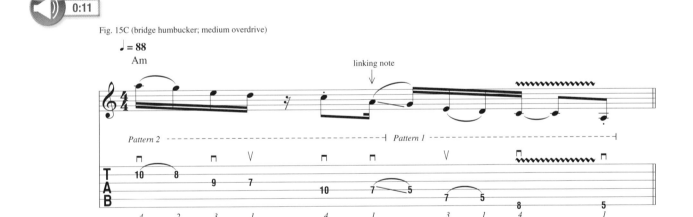

Fig. 15C (bridge humbucker; medium overdrive)

TRACK 15
0:21

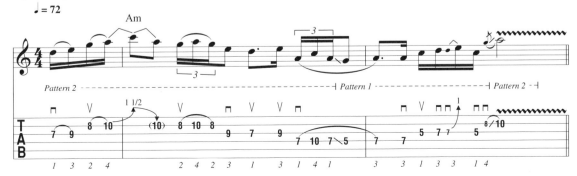

Fig. 15D (bridge humbucker; medium overdrive)

Connecting Pentatonic Patterns

Fig. 15E is influenced by Larry Carlton's silky phrasing in Steely Dan's "Kid Charlemagne." Start flattening out your index finger during the slide up to the 10th fret of the B string. That will put you nicely in the "saddle" for the ensuing double-stop slide. The riff-like moves in **Fig. 15F** are based on ex-Guns N' Roses guitarist Slash ("Welcome to the Jungle," "Sweet Child O' Mine"). Strive to let everything ring together by holding down all notes as long as possible. And try to keep your index finger barred across the D and G strings during the entire passage.

TRACK 15
0:35

Fig. 15E (neck humbucker; light overdrive)

TRACK 15
0:56

Fig. 15F (neck humbucker; medium/heavy overdrive)

It's back to blues with the example in **Fig. 15G,** where an array of double stops launches a passage that spills back and forth twice, between Pattern 2 and Pattern 1. Notice the jump from Pattern 2 back down to Pattern 1 at the closing moment of the phrase. Changing from one pattern to another without using a fretboard shift is called "jumping patterns."

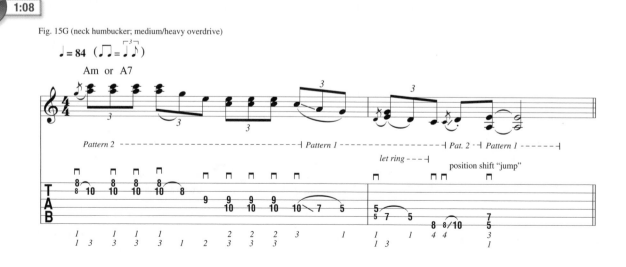

TRACK 15
1:08

Fig. 15G (neck humbucker; medium/heavy overdrive)

Solo 2A

Style: Blues Shuffle
Patterns: Pattern 1 and Pattern 2
Skill Level: Beginner/Intermediate

Solo 2A [**Fig. 16**] is performed over two choruses of a 12-bar blues in A (see Quick Theory Tutorial #4). This is a *dominant* blues, meaning all of the chords are dominant seventh in quality (R–3–5–♭7). The chord progression revolves around A7 (A–C♯–E–G), D7 (D–F♯–A–C), and E7 (E–G♯–B–D), with a passing F7 (F–A–C–E♭) in the final bar of each chorus. (See the chord frames at the top of the transcription for suggested voicings.) The groove is a medium shuffle, similar to "Pride and Joy" (Stevie Ray Vaughan) and "Sweet Home Chicago" (Robert Johnson).

Measures 1–12:

The solo opens with a set of licks in the "Albert King box" section of Pattern 2 (see Fig. 14D). Don't bend too sharp on the eighth-fret C notes; just a nudge will do. (For an explanation of the "pickup measure," refer to Fig. 14G.) In measure 3, the phrases start making their way down Pattern 2 with a variety of licks based on the ones explained in Figs. 14B–D. At measure 11, there's a jump (see Fig. 15G) down to Pattern 1, where a classic "turnaround lick" takes on the A7–F7–E7 changes. "Turnaround" refers to the last two measures in a 12-bar blues, where the progression "turns around," returning to the top of the form for another cycle. This turnaround lick encompasses many of the basic legato moves explained and demonstrated in the first section of this book (refer to "Pattern 1 Licks"). It's important to notice that the phrase ends on E (on the "and of 2" in measure 12), which is the root of the E7, or V chord. Many turnaround licks are crafted to hit, or "nail," the root of the V chord at the appropriate moment.

Measures 13–24:

At the top of the second chorus (or second time through the 12-bar form), a "call-and-response" theme is cast over measures 13–16. "Call and response" occurs when a lick is played, then answered by a similar or matching lick, and culminates with a conclusive, or resolving, phrase. Here, the "call" lick is measure 13, the "response" is in measure 14, and the "conclusion" is the long Pattern 2 phrase in measures 15–16. Incidentally, that series of hammer-on moves in measure 16 is sometimes referred to as the "Hideaway Lick," so called because the great Texas blues guitarist Freddie King featured it prominently in his classic tune, "Hideaway." Keep your index finger barred across the eighth fret of both the B and high-E strings for this lick.

Measures 17–18 feature moves explained in Figs. 14B–D, while measure 19 is a lot like the Don Felder maneuver from Fig. 15D. Measures 20–21 take a trip to the "cellar" with a position shift down into the lower extension box of Pattern 1 (see Figs. 8A–C), while the second half of measure 22 bears resemblance to the Larry Carlton-style lick from Fig. 15E. The "curtain closer" zips from pattern to pattern in a feisty lick brimming with bends, slides, and wicked vibrato. For the latter, pivot from the wrist, using an exaggerated up-and-down motion to repeatedly bend the string in quarter steps.

A good way to put this solo together is in two-bar increments. Once you have two measures down, move on to the next two-bar phrase. Then, go back and put them together in a four-bar phrase, and so on.

Quick Theory Tutorial #4

The 12-bar blues form is a 12-measure chord progression that is repeated through the course of a song. The most basic 12-bar blues form uses the I, IV, and V chords of the major scale (A, D, and E in the key of A major). Very often, these chords are converted to dominant seventh chords (A7–D7–E7). There are many variations on the 12-bar form, but a basic progression goes as follows: I chord (four measures), IV chord (two measures), I chord (two measures), V chord (one measure), IV chord (one measure), I chord (one measure), and V chord (one measure). Some famous examples of the 12-bar form include "Pride and Joy" (Stevie Ray Vaughan), "Crossroads" (Cream), "Johnny B. Goode" (Chuck Berry), and "Tush" (ZZ Top).

Tone Tips

Guitar: solidbody electric

Pickup Selection: neck

Pickup Type: humbucker

Gain: 4

EQ: Bass/Middle/Treble: 4/5/7

Effects: moderate reverb (small room)

Connecting Pentatonic Patterns

Fig. 16 "Solo 2A"

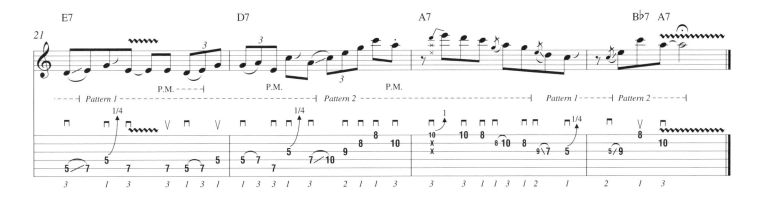

Solo 2B

Style: Blues Shuffle
Patterns: Pattern 1 and Pattern 2
Skill Level: Intermediate/Advanced

Solo 2B [**Fig. 17**] is, technically, a more challenging rendition of Solo 2A. Performed over the same progression and rhythm track, it ups the energy level with longer phrases, less space (rests), intense bends, and lots of double-stop passages.

Measures 1–12:

The solo opens with a call-and-response (see Fig. 16) passage spread out over the first four measures. Basically, a turbo-charged rendition of the lick in Fig. 15G, the segment opens with the "call" in measure 1 (double stops), followed by the "response" in measure 2 (variation of the call), and finishes with a two-bar "conclusion" (a standalone phrase containing elements of the first two licks) in measures 3–4. (Note the wide bend at the top of measure 4. Refer to Figs. 14F and 15D for details.)

Sliding 4ths (see Fig. 10K) is the theme of measures 5–6 (note the quick pattern segues), while 16th-note triplets highlight the Pattern 1/lower extension box handoff in measures 7–8 (see Fig. 8F). This sets off a triplet-fueled passage that snakes its way up Pattern 1, slides into Pattern 2, and the section goes out with a quarter note triplet-powered (three quarter notes in the space of two) variation on the opening phrase. Don't overlook the fact that the turnaround lick ends on E, the root of the V chord (see Fig. 16).

Measures 13–24:

The second chorus (second time through the form) opens with a double-stop passage played with caveman ferocity. (Listen to John Lennon's last solo break in the closing moments of the famous lead-guitar show-down in "The End," from the Beatles' *Abbey Road*.) Notice, once again, the call-and-response aspect of these two phrases (measures 13 and 14). Measure 15 hosts a smooth transition to Pattern 2, where another double-stop theme gradually gains momentum, escalating to an energetic repetition of 4ths dyads at the summit of Pattern 2.

Caution: brute strength is required in measure 19, where a set of Stevie Ray Vaughan-style double-stop bends (see Fig. 14E) result in a whole-step pitch modulation. (Don't worry if you can't match pitch exactly. As explained in Fig. 14E, pitches can vary greatly with this unique bending procedure.) Measure 21 features a classic "Albert King box" lick, where the G note is nudged up to hint at the 3rd (G♯) of the E7 chord. A blues "rake" (a quick strum, like a chord) up the top four-string set leads to a Jimi Hendrix-style, Pattern 2-to-Pattern 1 handoff, embellished with double-stop hammer-ons. The solo goes out with an active phrase that covers nearly the entire spectrum of Pattern 2.

> ## Tone Tips
> **Guitar:** solidbody electric
>
> **Pickup Selection:** neck
>
> **Pickup Type:** humbucker
>
> **Gain:** 4
>
> **EQ: Bass/Middle/Treble:** 4/5/7
>
> **Effects:** moderate reverb (small room)

Connecting Pentatonic Patterns

Fig. 17 "Solo 2B"

CHAPTER 3

PATTERN 3:
Juggling Patterns 1, 2, and 3

This chapter introduces Pattern 3 of the minor pentatonic scale; techniques for connecting it with Pattern 2; and methods for combining—or juggling—Patterns 1, 2, and 3.

Pattern 3 of the A Minor Pentatonic Scale

The neck diagrams in **Fig. 18A** illustrate Pattern 3 of the A minor pentatonic scale. The lowest root (A) is at the 12th fret of the A string, the octave is at the 10th fret of the B string, and the highest note in the pattern is E, the 5th of the scale. The lowest note in the pattern (D, the 4th of the scale) is at the 10th fret of the low-E string. Remember, this is a movable pattern. For instance, if you wanted to use this to play the E minor pentatonic scale (E–G–A–B–D), you would simply slide the pattern down the neck until the root aligns with E on the fretboard—the seventh fret of the A string.

Of the five patterns of the minor pentatonic scale, Pattern 3 has the widest spread—a five-fret jump between the ninth fret (G string) and the 13th fret (B string)—on the fretboard. This makes it rather difficult to master and may take some getting used to. The lower portion (notes on the low-E, A, and D strings) is very symmetrical and easily navigated, but the top three strings contain some rather scattered moves.

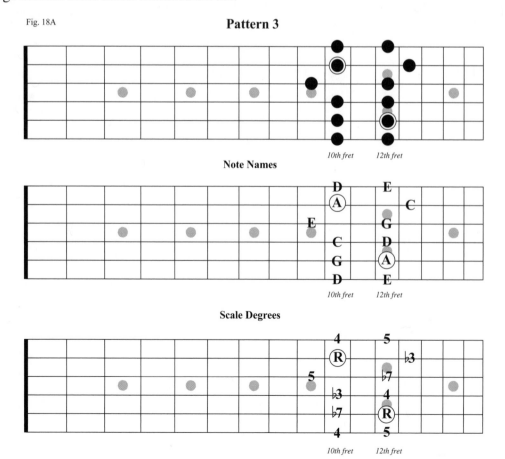

Fig. 18A   **Pattern 3**

10th fret   12th fret

Note Names

10th fret   12th fret

Scale Degrees

10th fret   12th fret

Fig. 18B offers some fingering suggestions for both ascending and descending the scale. Play through the pattern (starting from the root, as in the example) with the first finger suggestions, and then with the other. Also, take the time to "burn in" little sections of the pattern. For instance, go up and down the low three-string set for a while, seeing what interesting melodies you come up with. You may also want to run up and down the "inner octave" portion of the scale pattern, from the root on the A string to the octave on the B string, over and over. While you're at it, try transferring some of the Pattern 1 and Pattern 2 licks from the previous chapters to this pattern!

TRACK 18

Fig. 18B

Licks Crafted From Pattern 3

Fig. 19A exploits the symmetrical properties of the low string set (all notes are on the 10th and 12th frets) with a two-finger legato lick. If only all scale passages on the guitar were as easy to play!

TRACK 19   0:00

Fig. 19A (bridge humbucker; medium overdrive)

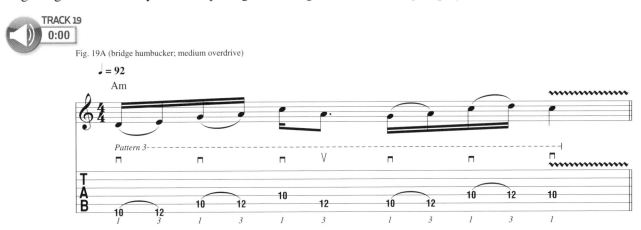

Fig. 19B manipulates this same area with a descending passage that ends in a string jump (see Fig. 6E). By the way, if this six-note sequence feels familiar, that's because it's the same collection of notes (and pattern) as the one found on the A, D, and G strings of Pattern 1 (see Fig. 2).

TRACK 19   0:09

Fig. 19B (neck single coil; light overdrive)

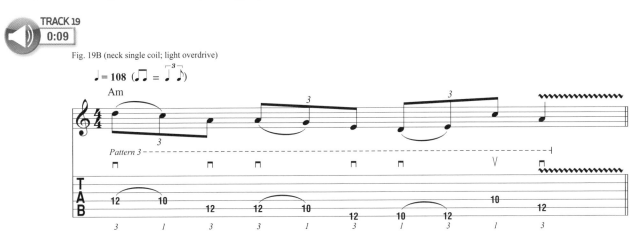

Connecting Pentatonic Patterns

Fig. 19C is, essentially, an ascending lick that hits almost every note of the pattern. Adding vibrato to the E/C dyad may be a bit of a challenge. Classical (side-to-side motion) vibrato might be the easiest, but if you want to employ a blues-rock vibrato (bending up and down), be sure to keep the strings parallel to each other.

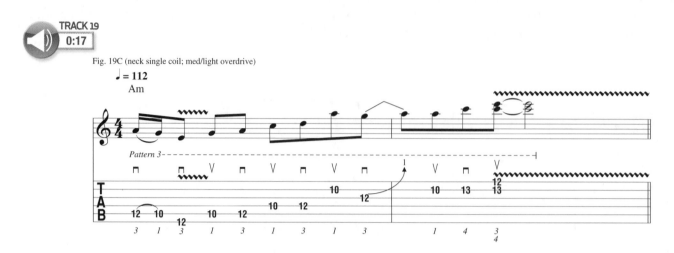

TRACK 19
0:17

Fig. 19C (neck single coil; med/light overdrive)

Fig. 19D is a funky, arpeggiated lick (it spells out an Am7 arpeggio: A–C–E–G) that uses *syncopation* (i.e., surprise or unexpected rhythms that accent the upbeat) to add interest to the line. The first set of notes involves a "slow rake," whereby the pick is dragged in one direction across consecutive strings.

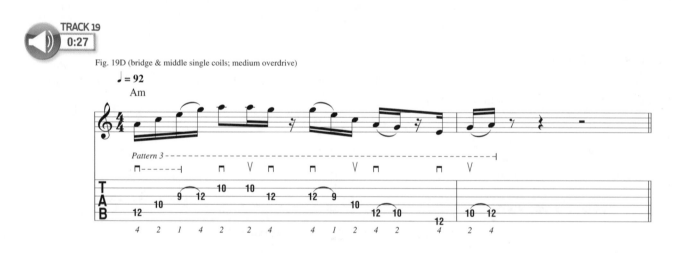

TRACK 19
0:27

Fig. 19D (bridge & middle single coils; medium overdrive)

Fig. 19E is a speedy lick that cascades down Pattern 3 in sequential segments (see Figs. 4A–E). The "hand scrunch" indicators refer to the physical act of "scrunching" the fretting hand to facilitate the tight fingering moves.

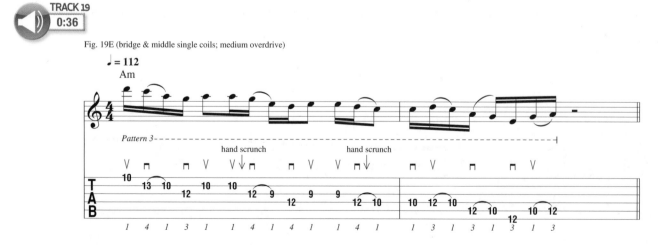

TRACK 19
0:36

Fig. 19E (bridge & middle single coils; medium overdrive)

The "bendy" example in **Fig. 19F** is related to Fig. 5C from Chapter 1. You may notice that it's somewhat easier to bend the strings in the upper portions of the fretboard. That's because you don't have to apply as much bending pressure to achieve the same pitch alteration.

TRACK 19
0:54

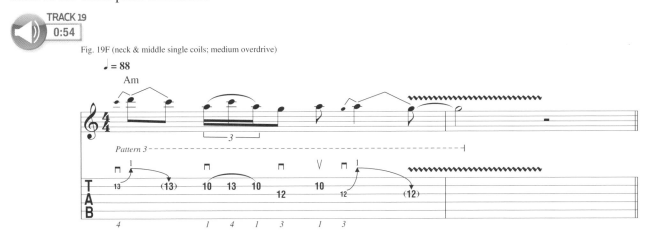

Fig. 19F (neck & middle single coils; medium overdrive)

Fig. 19G is a "fixed string" bend. Begin by planting your ring (3rd) and pinky (4th) fingers on the 12th and 13th frets of the G and B strings, respectively. Now strike the G string and bend up a whole step. While holding the bend, strike the B-string note, letting it sustain while you strike the G string again and release the bend. This type of bend is sometimes called a "pedal steel" bend because it emulates the sound of the pedal steel guitar licks from country music. Country pickers such as Jerry Donahue, Brad Paisley, and Brent Mason excel at these types of licks, but rockers such as Jimmy Page, Slash, and Zakk Wylde also like to throw these types of moves into their solos.

TRACK 19
1:04

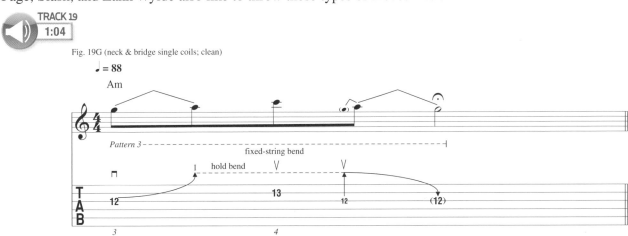

Fig. 19G (neck & bridge single coils; clean)

Fig. 19H scoots across Pattern 3 via a three-note legato motif—a hammer-on move on the lower string, followed by one note on the adjacent, higher string. **Fig. 19I** is a fiery, song-capping lick reminiscent of Jimmy Page (Led Zeppelin) or Lynyrd Skynyrd's classic guitar team, Gary Rossington and Allen Collins. The lick culminates in another type of fixed-string bend called a "unison bend." Also referred to as an "oblique bend," a unison bend involves bending the G string note up a whole step to match the pitch of the fretted B-string note. Don't worry much about matching pitch exactly—sometimes the warbling dissonance adds the perfect blues-rock touch.

TRACK 19
1:14

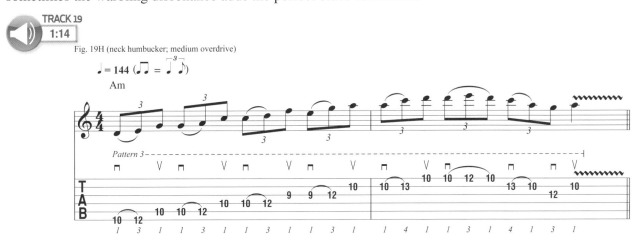

Fig. 19H (neck humbucker; medium overdrive)

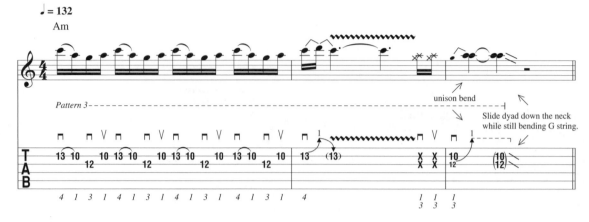

Fig. 19I (bridge humbucker; heavy overdrive)

Lining Up Patterns 1, 2, and 3

Fig. 20A lines up Patterns 1, 2, and 3 of the A minor pentatonic scale along the fretboard. Dashed lines are used to mark the borders of Patterns 1 and 3, while a solid line outlines Pattern 2. Again, notice the similarity to puzzle pieces, in that the patterns sort of "snap" together, joining at their junctions with shared linking notes.

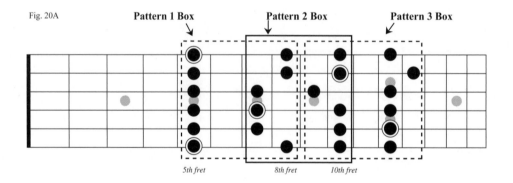

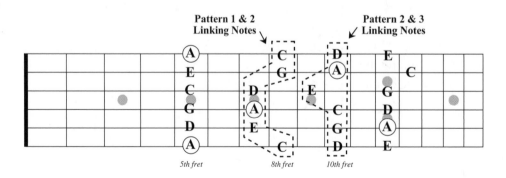

Juggling Patterns 1, 2, and 3

Here are some examples that toss the patterns about, like a circus performer might juggle bowling pins. The lick in **Fig. 20B** slides up the neck by skirting along the lower edges of Patterns 1, 2, and 3. You'll need to use a "hand scrunch" (see Fig. 19E) to grab that 10th-fret G note on beat 3.

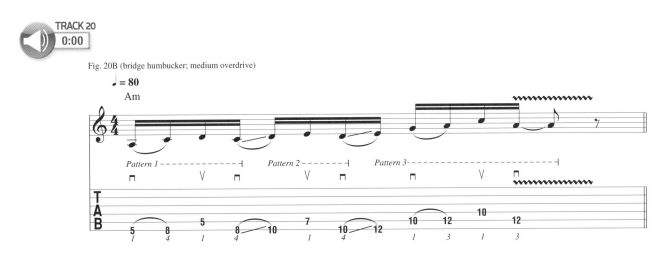

Fig. 20B (bridge humbucker; medium overdrive)

Fig. 20C makes its way down the neck via the B and G string sets of Patterns 1, 2, and 3. Pay strict attention to the picking directions and fingering suggestions in this example.

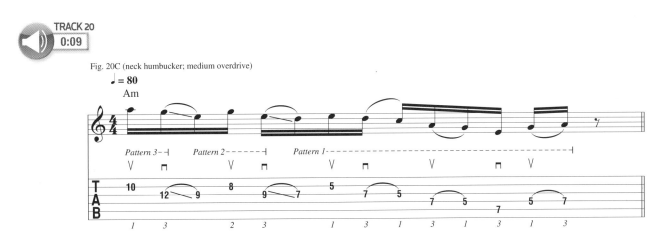

Fig. 20C (neck humbucker; medium overdrive)

Fig. 20D is a rather complex lick that is easier to tackle if broken down into segments. Notice that the lick begins in the "Albert King box" section of Pattern 2 (see Figs. 7A, 13A, and 14D). From there, it slides up to Pattern 3, where it spins out two short phrases, then segues down into Pattern 2 again for a descending line, whereupon it toggles back to Pattern 3 for the final notes of the passage.

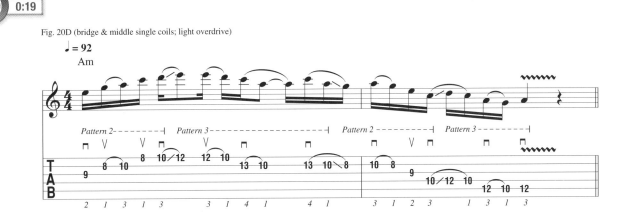

Fig. 20D (bridge & middle single coils; light overdrive)

Connecting Pentatonic Patterns

Fig. 20E is a double-stop-fueled passage isolated on the top three string set of all three patterns. The moves in each box are very similar, so make sure that you have the first part of the phrase down (Pattern 1) before moving on to the rest of the example. If you feel like you need some guidance with fret-hand maneuvering, refer back to Chapter 1 (Figs. 6A–D).

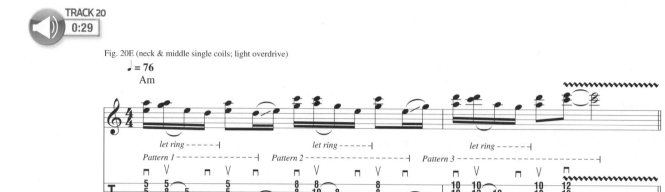

Fig. 20F is an interesting example that crosses a large portion of each pattern as it makes its way down the fretboard. Notice that the melody in measure 1 is transposed down an octave in measure 2.

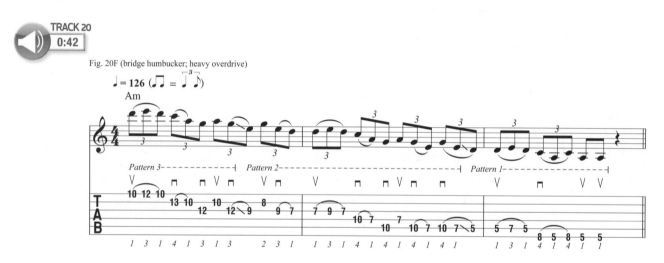

Solo 3A

Style: Funk-Rock
Patterns: Pattern 1, Pattern 2, and Pattern 3
Skill Level: Beginner/Intermediate

Solo 3A [**Fig. 21**] is performed in a funk-rock vein. Twenty-four measures in length, it is divided into three eight-bar sections. The first of these sections (measures 1–8) revolves around an Am7–Em7 vamp, or im7–vm7 in the key of A minor (refer to Quick Theory Tutorial #5). The only change in the cycle is in measures 4 and 8, where a C (♭III) chord gives way to a D (IV) chord. (Incidentally, the D chord is like an adjustment of the true harmony of the iv chord, which is Dm. This is a common occurrence in all styles of music and is sometimes referred to as *modal interchange*.) The second section (measures 9–16) is based on a ♭VI–♭VII–im7 cadence (again, refer to Quick Theory Tutorial #5), which is cycled three times, with the exception of the D chord in measure 14. This section closes with a ♭III–♭VII (C–G) handoff, followed by a quick i–♭VII–v (Am–G–Em) wrap-up. The final section (measures 17–24) is identical to the first section, except for the last two measures, which are adjusted to resolve on the i (Am) chord.

Quick Theory Tutorial #5

Minor scale harmony refers to the process of putting specific minor scale tones together to create chords. For example, the A minor scale is: A–B–C–D–E–F–G. And, in scale formula terminology, it reads: 1–2–♭3–4–5–♭6–♭7. Grouping the 1st, ♭3rd, and 5th tones (in other words, every other note) of the scale (A–C–E) creates an Am chord. This is called the *triad harmony* of the i (pronounced "one") chord. Add the ♭7th of the scale (G) to the triad and you get an Am7 (A–C–E–G) chord. This is the *seventh chord harmony* of the root of the scale, and is symbolized as "im7." Continuing this process with each scale degree results in the following triads: Am–B°–C–Dm–Em–F–G. In Roman numeral terminology, this reads: i–ii°–♭III–iv–v–♭VI–♭VII. The seventh chord harmony of the A minor scale is Am7–Bm7♭5–Cmaj7–Dm7–Em7–Fmaj7–G7. And in Roman numerals: im7–iim7♭5–♭IIImaj7–ivm7–vm7–♭VImaj7–♭VII7. (For an in-depth study on scale harmony, refer to the suggested companion book *Music Theory for Guitarists: Everything You Ever Wanted to Know but Were Afraid to Ask* [Hal Leonard].)

Measures 1–8:

The solo opens with a set of pickup notes (see Fig. 14G) that dash up the lower region of Pattern 3. Remaining in this same area for nearly two measures, the phrasing then slithers down the low-E string (Pattern 2) to briefly settle into Pattern 1 (measure 3 and top of measure 4). Here, the lick from Fig. 20B is called to action for a three-pattern handoff that climbs the fretboard, courtesy of a two-16ths/eighth-note rhythmic motif (measure 4). At this point, we stay put in Pattern 3 for the remainder of the section (measures 5–8). Highlights include the bluesy half-step bend on the 12th fret of the D string (D bent to E♭) in measure 5, the whole-step bends on the 12th fret of the G string (G bent to A) in measures 6 and 7, and the rhythmic motif action in measures 7 and 8 (four 16th notes followed by two eighths).

Measures 9–16:

Measure 9 heralds the change to the chord progression, whereupon a rhythmically matched set of licks makes its way up the midsections of Patterns 1, 2, and 3. Measures 10–13 host a collection of intriguing moves, all cut from Pattern 3. Measure 10 is a variation on the opening melody (pickup notes and first part of measure 1), measure 11 contains some non-diatonic (outside of the scale) grace-note slides, and the goings-on in measures 12–13 illustrate how some Pattern 1 licks can be directly transported to Pattern 3 with positive results! (Compare the similarities of these measures to the Pattern 1 licks in Figs. 5B–C.) All of the slip-slidey maneuvers in the remaining measures of this section (14–16) draw from the pattern-juggling tactics in Fig. 20C. As with that lick, proper fingering and picking directions are crucial for a smooth outcome.

Measures 17–24:

Section 3 opens with a strong rhythmic theme that is carried out across measures 17 and 18. Notice that the phrasing starts out in the lower extension box of Pattern 1 (refer to Fig. 7A). The lick in measure 19 is cast from the example explained in Fig. 20D, and measure 20 has its origins in the "transported lick" concept described in measures 12–13 above. "Backwards slides" (themselves, powerful guitar nuances) provide the pattern handoffs in measures 21–22, and the solo goes out with a neck-climbing lick this is bookended by double stops. Be careful here—this passage requires some tricky fingering. Take it slowly and follow the fingering suggestions carefully.

Tone Tips

Guitar: solidbody electric

Pickup Selection: bridge and middle

Pickup Type: single coils

Gain: 4

EQ: Bass/Middle/Treble: 5/4/6

Effects: moderate reverb (hall), moderate delay with long slap (approx. 650ms)

Connecting Pentatonic Patterns

Fig. 21 "Solo 3A"

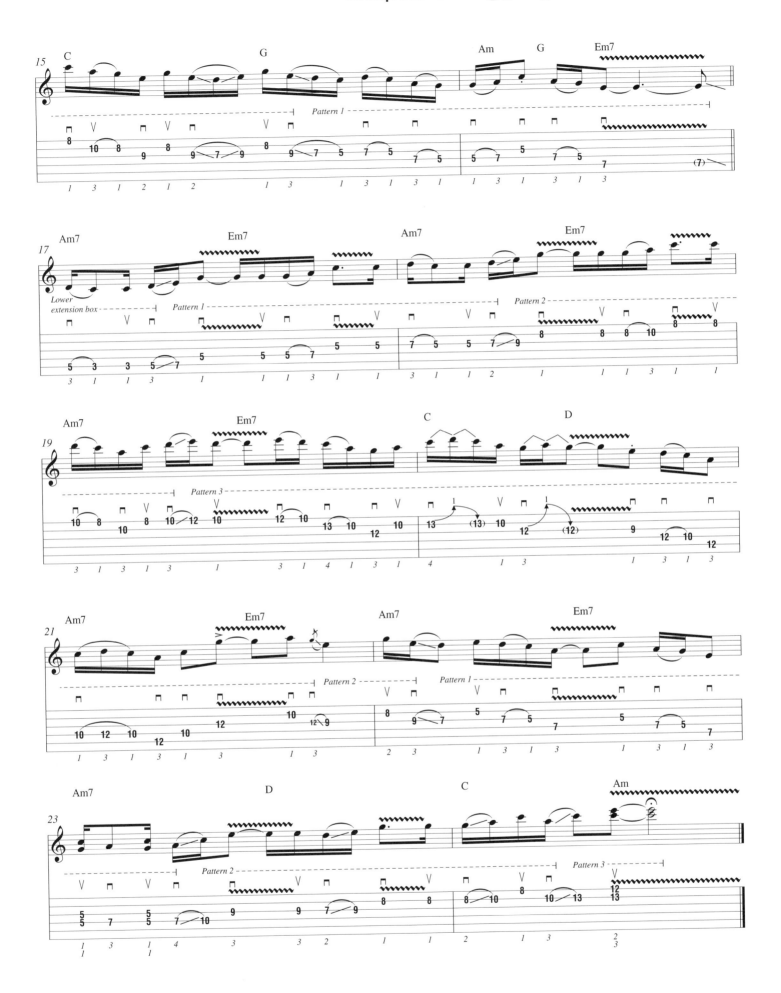

Solo 3B

Style: Funk-Rock
Patterns: Pattern 1, Pattern 2, and Pattern 3
Skill Level: Intermediate/Advanced

The intensity factor is ratcheted up substantially in Solo 3B [**Fig. 22**]. Performed over the same rhythm track as Solo 3A, it is technically more advanced and demanding due to its non-stop energy.

Measures 1–8:

The solo opens with a barrage of double stops voiced on the top regions of Patterns 2 and 3 (see Fig. 20E). Measures 2–3 witness some "pattern juggling" maneuvers (back and forth between Pattern 2 and 3), and measure 4 features a low-E string descent replete with a series of dead-note inflections (see Fig. 3A for explanation) that up the funk factor. Measures 5–6 house an aggressively picked passage that requires the fret-hand muting techniques explained in Fig. 14H, and measures 7–8 close the section with a full-circle return to the high-voiced double stops in Patterns 2 and 3.

Measures 9–16:

The section opens with a variation on the Jimmy Page-style lick described in Fig. 19I (albeit slower and funkier), followed by an Am7 arpeggio lick (see Fig. 19D) in measure 10, which spills into a "Hideaway"-style lick (refer to measure 16 of Solo 2A) at the top of measure 11. The incendiary lick in measure 12 is essentially a supercharged rendition of Fig. 19H. Proper picking direction is the prime directive here. A passing open B-string attack precedes another set of transported Pattern 1 licks (see measures 12–13 of Solo 3A), and the section goes out with an extended phrase on the lower string set of Pattern 3 (see Figs. 19A–B).

Measures 17–24:

Measure 17 sparks an ambitious double-stop rally that rises and falls over the course of five full measures (bars 17–21). At first glance, the phrase may seem a bit daunting, but all of these moves have been discussed in previous examples. If you need guidance, refer to Figs. 6A–D, 8E, 9E, 10J–K, and 20E. Don't get too hung up with the rhythmic notation in measure 22; it's simply a four-note lick propelled by a triple stop (three-note chord) that is repeated four times. The kicker is that each time the lick is repeated, it accelerates in tempo (be sure to listen to the audio demonstration). The solo goes out on a two-bar neck-climbing lick that is based on the principals of Fig. 9F.

Tone Tips

Guitar: solidbody electric

Pickup Selection: bridge and middle

Pickup Type: single coils

Gain: 5

EQ: Bass/Middle/Treble: 3/4/7

Effects: moderate reverb (hall), moderate delay with long slap (approx. 650ms)

TRACK 22

Fig. 22 "Solo 3B"

Connecting Pentatonic Patterns

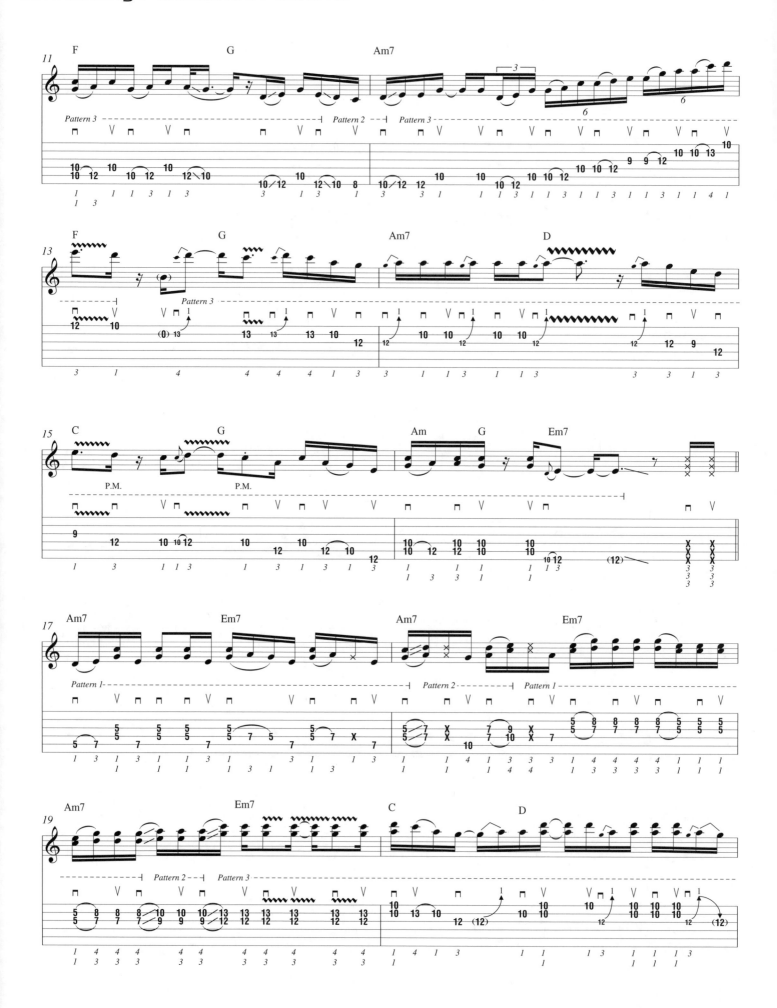

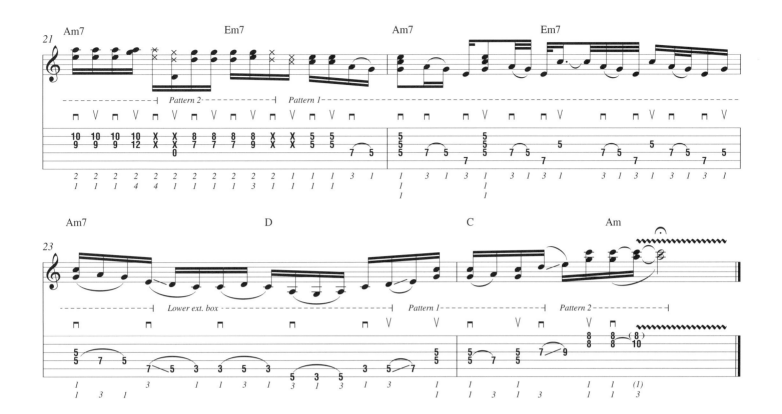

CHAPTER 4

PATTERN 4:
Connecting, Transferring, and Transposing Patterns

This chapter introduces Pattern 4 of the minor pentatonic scale, as well as licks derived from the pattern and techniques for connecting it to Pattern 3. Also included are methods for transposing licks from pattern to pattern and to other keys, as well.

Pattern 4 of the A Minor Pentatonic Scale

Fig. 23A illustrates Pattern 4 of the A minor pentatonic scale. Again, the top neck diagram depicts the note placement, the middle diagram shows the note names, and the bottom neck indicates the scale degrees. As you can see, the first octave of the pattern (A–C–D–E–G–A) is similar in structure to Pattern 1. Be careful when you move to the B string, though, as it's easy to make a mistake and go for the 12th fret instead of the 13th! Use the fingering suggestions in **Fig. 23B** to practice playing through the pattern.

Fig. 23A

Pattern 4

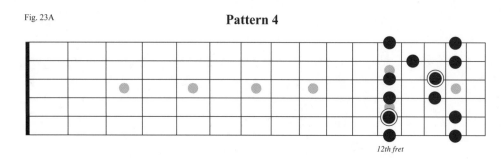

12th fret

Note Names

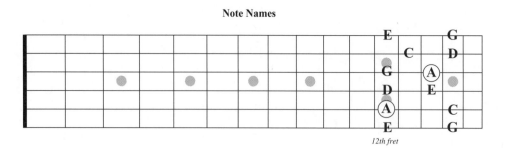

12th fret

Scale Degrees

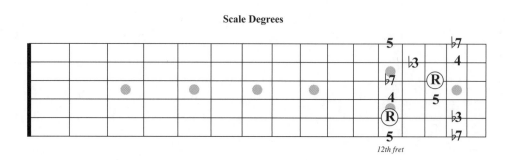

12th fret

TRACK 23

Fig. 23B

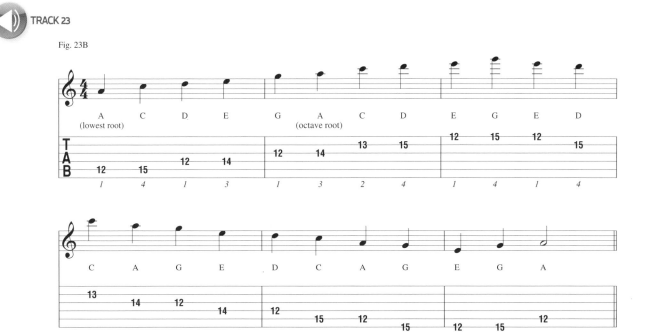

Transferring Licks from Pattern 1

Pattern 4 is a popular pattern for pentatonic players of all styles. Likely, this is because it is so similar in shape to the "primary" pentatonic box—Pattern 1. In many cases, the similar structures make it easy to transfer, or transpose, Pattern 1 licks up an octave, to Pattern 4. Here are a few examples to help demonstrate the process.

Fig. 24A takes the lick from Fig. 3A and transposes it up an octave, to Pattern 4. Notice that, although the lick is played on different strings, the fret-hand fingering is identical up until you get to the B string.

TRACK 24
0:00

Fig. 24A (bridge humbucker; medium overdrive)

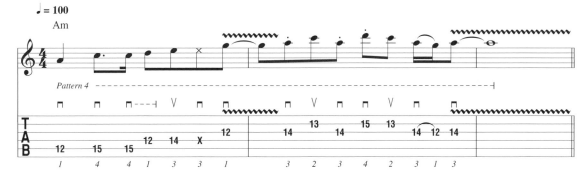

Fig. 24B transfers the Pattern 1 lick in Fig. 3D to Pattern 4. Again, notice the similarity in fingering.

TRACK 24
0:13

Fig. 24B (bridge humbucker; medium overdrive)

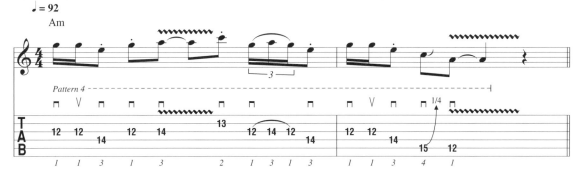

Fig. 24C takes the funky example in Fig. 3F and transposes it up an octave, to Pattern 4. The highest note (A) is out of the pattern, but the pitch is obtained by bending G (on the high-E string) up a whole step.

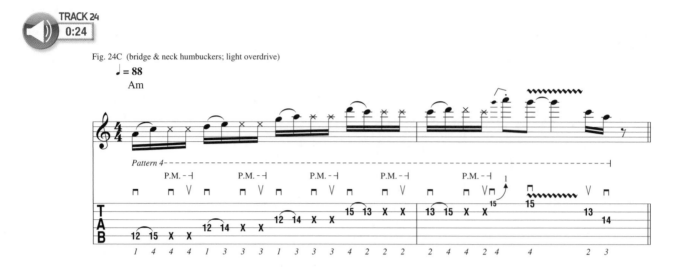

Fig. 24C (bridge & neck humbuckers; light overdrive)

Fig. 24D takes the "bendy" lick from Fig. 5A and moves it up an octave, to Pattern 4. Make sure that you line up your other fingers along the string (behind the bending fret, toward the headstock) and use them to help in the bending chores.

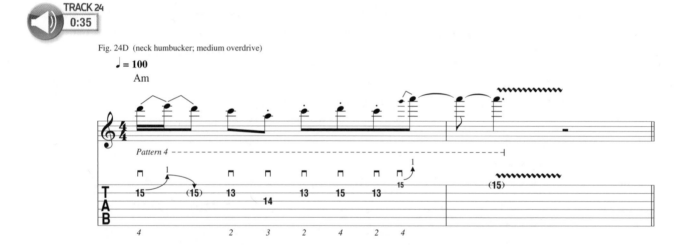

Fig. 24D (neck humbucker; medium overdrive)

Transposing Licks to Other Keys

Don't forget that all of the Patterns we've covered are movable to any key (see Chapter 1, Fig. 2). (This book has stated this fact all along, but for the sake of continuity and clarity, the primary focus has been on the A minor pentatonic scale.) **Fig. 25A** on the following page offers an example of transposing an A minor pentatonic lick, using Pattern 1. The chord progression is Am–Dm–Em–Am, or i–iv–v–i in the key of A minor (see Quick Theory Tutorial #5, in Chapter 3). Since all of the chords belong to the key of A minor, the A minor pentatonic scale could be used throughout the progression. However, this example starts with an A minor pentatonic phrase for the Am chord, then transposes it to the D minor pentatonic scale (D–F–G–A–C) for the Dm chord, and the E minor pentatonic scale (E–G–A–B–D) for the Em chord. The process is really quite simple: the A minor pentatonic lick in measure 1 is crafted from Pattern 1. In measure 2, the lick is transposed by simply shifting it up the fretboard to align with Pattern 1 of the D minor pentatonic scale at the 10th fret. In measure 3, the lick is moved two frets higher (12th fret) for transposition to the E minor pentatonic scale. Measure 4 moves back to Pattern 1 of the A minor pentatonic scale.

Fig. 25A (neck humbucker; light overdrive)

Fig. **25B** remaps the licks in Fig. 25A so the moves won't be so "jumpy." Measures 1 and 4 are played in the same area as before, but the D minor and E minor pentatonic phrases are directly transferred (in the same octave) to Pattern 4. Notice that this process consolidates all of the moves to a more compact section of the fretboard.

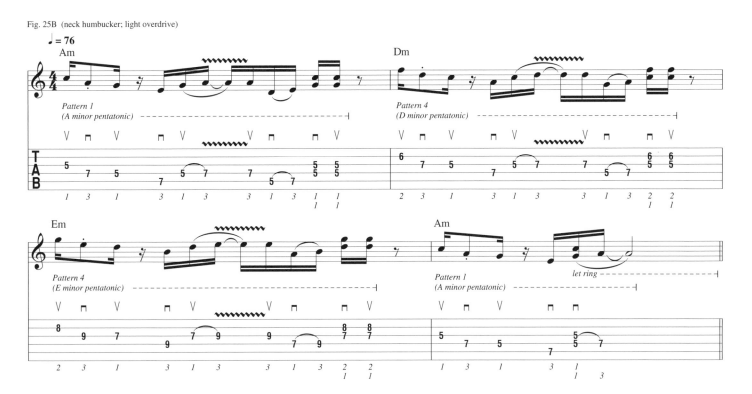

Fig. 25B (neck humbucker; light overdrive)

Standalone Pattern 4 Licks

Here are a few licks that showcase the finger-friendly properties of Pattern 4. **Fig. 26A** is a bluesy lick that features a fixed-string bend (see Fig. 19G) on the high string set. Be sure to keep the note on the high-E string stationary as you bend the B string to pitch. **Fig. 26B** is a lick that exploits the symmetrical properties of the low-E and A strings (i.e., the notes are on the same frets of both strings). The example in **Fig. 26C** features a common move in many hard-rock solos: a cycled trio of notes on the top two strings. **Fig. 26D** uses the legato motif introduced in Fig. 19H to zoom up Pattern 4. Be careful—this one starts with a pickup note. **Fig. 26E** is an Am7 arpeggio (A–C–E–G) lick that ends with a minor pentatonic run. Follow the picking directions carefully.

Fig. 26A (neck humbucker; medium overdrive)

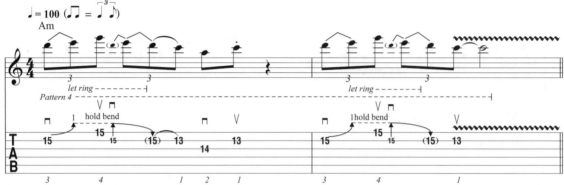

Fig. 26B (bridge & middle single coils; medium overdrive)

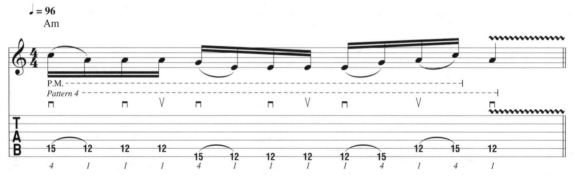

Fig. 26C (bridge humbucker; heavy overdrive)

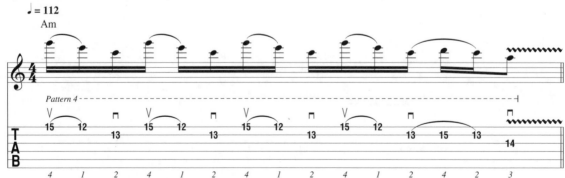

TRACK 26
0:34

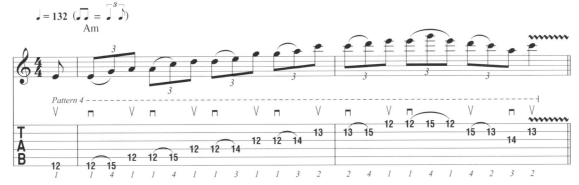

Fig. 26D (bridge humbucker; heavy overdrive)

TRACK 26
0:53

Fig. 26E (neck single coil; heavy overdrive)

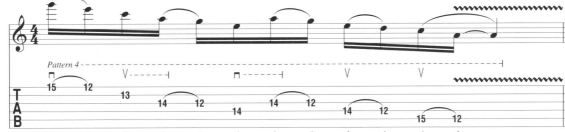

Snapping Patterns 1, 2, 3, and 4 into Place

The top neck diagram in **Fig. 27A** illustrates how Patterns 1, 2, 3, and 4 of the A minor pentatonic scale connect on the fretboard. Pattern 4 is at the top of the neck (12th fret) and is outlined with a solid black line. Just below that is Pattern 3 (indicated with dashed lines), then Pattern 2 (solid black-line border), and, lastly, Pattern 1 (dashed-line border). Again, try to envision the boxes as pieces of a jigsaw puzzle that "snap" together along the fretboard. The neck diagram at the bottom of Fig. 27A illustrates the linking notes, where the patterns join together.

Fig. 27A

A Minor Pentatonic Scale

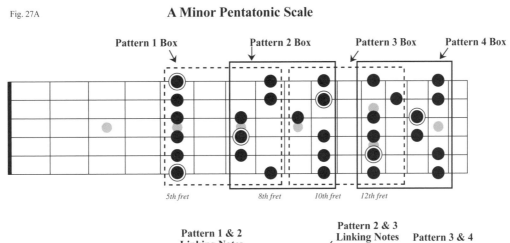

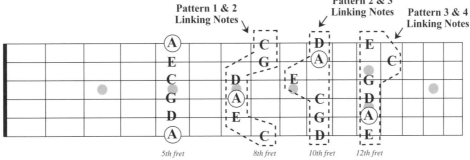

Connecting Licks

Fig. 27B is a Clapton-esque lick that starts in Pattern 4, then spills into Pattern 3. The double-stop action in **Fig. 27C** is reminiscent of Jimi Hendrix and Stevie Ray Vaughan's solo work. Notice in both of these licks that Pattern 3 serves as the lower extension box for Pattern 4. The lick in **Fig. 27D** skips along the middle string set (D and G strings) of all four patterns like a little kid playing hopscotch. If you keep your ring (3rd) finger glued to the D string throughout the lick, you should be fine.

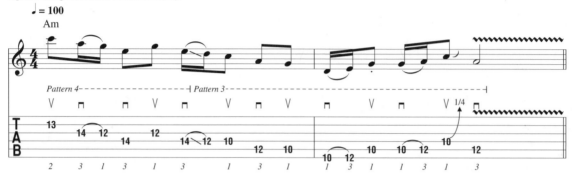

Fig. 27B (bridge humbucker; medium overdrive)

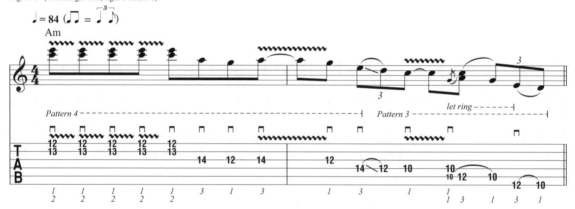

Fig. 27C (neck single coil; light overdrive)

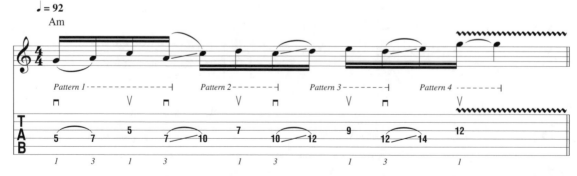

Fig. 27D (bridge humbucker; medium overdrive)

Fig. 27E has its roots in the melodic-motif, string-skipping lick in Fig. 9C from Chapter 1. A three-note "hammer-on/ adjacent-string" pattern is launched in Pattern 1, and then gradually morphs into a slide/string-jump move that crosses the upper Patterns (2, 3, and 4).

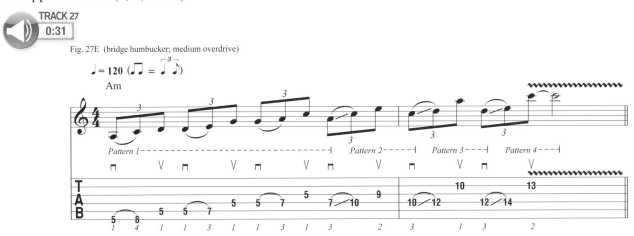

Fig. 27E (bridge humbucker; medium overdrive)

Fig. 27F "ping-pongs" and cascades down Patterns 3 and 4 in measure 1 via a two-fingered power-chord shape. Hitting the low string set in measure 2, the shape slithers down the neck, visiting the bottom portions of each Pattern. Be sure to hit the 15th fret (instead of the "expected" 14th fret) of the A string in measure 2. The final note (A on the low-E string) requires a "pattern jump," instead of a slide. Keep your index finger lightly touching the low-E string as you make the jump from the eighth fret to the fifth-fret finish line.

Fig. 27F (bridge humbucker; heavy overdrive)

The challenging example in **Fig. 27G** travels full circle from Pattern 4, down to Pattern 1, and back up again to the starting point. The lick starts with an Am7 arpeggio (A–C–E–G) that is played with a technique known as *sweep picking*. Sweep picking involves using a single downstroke (or upstroke) to pick notes on a consecutive set of strings. From there, the lick travels down Patterns 3 and 2 courtesy of the adjacent-string "hopscotch" maneuver introduced in Fig. 27D. Upon hitting Pattern 1, the phrase falls down the scale, and then travels back up to Pattern 4 along the low-E and A string set.

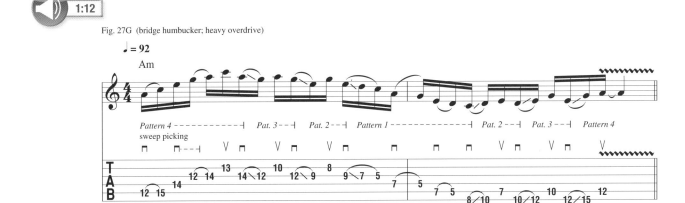

Fig. 27G (bridge humbucker; heavy overdrive)

Connecting Pentatonic Patterns

Fig. 27H is an inventive lick that is loosely based on scale harmony (refer to Quick Theory Tutorial #5, in Chapter 3). This particular method involves arpeggiating three-note "chord shapes" crafted from pentatonic patterns. This example starts with three selected notes from Pattern 1 (fifth fret of the A string, seventh fret of the D string, and fifth fret of the B string). Each note is then moved up the fretboard to its corresponding "diatonic" location in Pattern 2. (Essentially, each note ascends to the next scale degree of the A minor pentatonic scale.) Once there, the notes are repositioned to Pattern 3, and finally to Pattern 4. (The chord names above the staff indicate the resultant chord harmonies.) Eric Johnson pushes the envelope of complexity with similar moves in his tour de force, "Cliffs of Dover."

TRACK 27
1:35

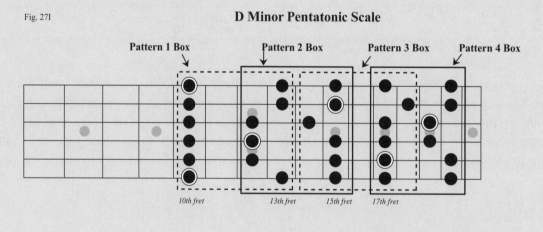

Quick Theory Tutorial #6

Quick Theory Tutorial #1 (Chapter 1) explained that the A minor pentatonic scale (A–C–D–E–G) is derived from the A natural minor scale (A–B–C–D–E–F–G) by omitting the 2nd and ♭6th scale degrees (B and F). The same holds true for the D minor pentatonic scale (D–F–G–A–C), which is derived from the D natural minor scale (D–E–F–G–A–B♭–C). Again, the 2nd and ♭6th degrees (E and B♭) are omitted to form its minor pentatonic counterpart. Memorizing the notes of the minor pentatonic scale in every key is a daunting task, but transposing pentatonic scale patterns on the fretboard can be much less complicated. For example, **Fig. 27I** lays out Patterns 1–4 of the D minor pentatonic scale in the top neck diagram. Compare this illustration to the A minor pentatonic boxes in Fig. 27A and you'll see that they're identical. The only difference is that the D minor pentatonic lineup starts at the 10th fret. (The boxes in the lower neck diagram identify the scale notes.)

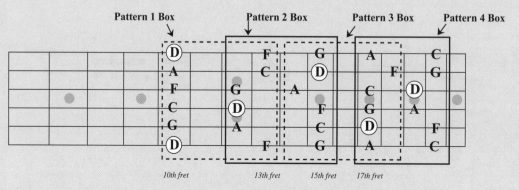

Fig. 27I — D Minor Pentatonic Scale

Solo 4A

Style: Uptempo Hard Rock
Scales/Patterns:
> A Minor Pentatonic: Patterns 1, 2, 3, and 4
> D Minor Pentatonic: Patterns 1 and 2

Skill Level: Intermediate

Clocking in at a whopping 40 measures, Solo 4A [**Fig. 28**] is the longest yet encountered in this book. But like the other solos, it's much easier to tackle when broken down into sections. (Note: this transcription includes section letters.)

Although it looks a bit complex, Section A (measures 1–8) can be analyzed as i–♭III–♭VII–i (Am–C–G–Am) in the key of A minor (see Quick Theory Tutorial #5). Viewing the Am7 (A–C–E–G) and Am9 (A–C–E–G–B) chords as simply colorful versions of Am, the progression reads: i (four bars), ♭III (one bar), ♭VII (one bar), and i (two bars). (The ♭VII chord is actually anticipated, occurring on beat 4 of its preceding measure.) Section B (measures 9–16) is the same progression as Section A.

Section C (measures 17–32) temporarily modulates to the key of D minor (see Quick Theory Tutorial #6) for four measures via a i-chord vamp that involves Dm and C/D (D9sus4) chords (see the voicings at the top of transcription). It's tempting to analyze this modulation as the iv chord in A minor, but the change is extended across four measures— enough time to argue an actual key change. At measure 21, the progression reverts back to the original key of A minor, revisiting the i-chord vamp (Am9–Am7–Am) from the previous sections. At measure 25, it's back again to the key of D minor (Dm–C/D chord vamp) for the remainder of the section (measures 25–32).

Section D (measures 33–40) returns to the key of A minor. The first four measures mirror the first half of Section A, while the final four measures involve a "modal" treatment of the Am chord, whereby a series of major triads are cast over a droning A tonic note (see the voicings at the top of the transcription).

A Section (measures 1–8):

The solo opens on a series of blues-rock phrases cast from Patterns 4 and 3. Scattered across the fertile area described in Fig. 27A, the licks are founded on eighth-note rhythms, accelerating to 16th notes in the last two measures. Don't over-look the subtle, but effective, legato nuances: vibrato on sustained notes (bars 1, 3, 5, and 7); quarter-step bends (measures 2 and 6); and pattern-shifting grace-note slides (bars 3 and 5). Also take notice of the use of space (rests between phrases) in measures 4, 6, and 8.

B Section (measures 9–16):

Speedy legato maneuvers in the "symmetrical box" portion of Pattern 3 (see Figs. 18A and 19A) open the B section with a bang! (This phrase actually starts with the pickup notes in the last measure of the A section.) In measure 10, a Pattern 4 lick serves as a response, followed by a brief handoff to Pattern 3, and the section goes out with an extended stay in the upper portion of Pattern 4. Note the inclusion of 12th-fret dyads that were introduced in Fig. 27C and the high-E and B-string bends first encountered in Figs. 24C–D.

C Section (measures 17–32):

The C section brings the D minor key change (see analysis above) and the phrasing nestles into Pattern 1 of the D minor pentatonic scale. Don't be confused here—this four-bar section (measures 17–20) uses the same Pattern 1 phrasing elements explained in Chapter 1 of this book (see Figs. 3A–G, 4A–G, 5A–F, and 6A–F). The only difference is that the Pattern is relocated (transposed) to the 10th fret.

At measure 21, it's back to the original key of A minor, and the solo slips effortlessly into the Pattern 4 region of A minor pentatonic for four measures (21–24). Be careful with that pre-bend figure in measure 23—it's pretty intense! Bend with your pinky, but line up your other digits along the string (12th–14th fret area) to help push the note up to pitch. Measure 25 modulates back to the key of D minor and the solo follows suit with a quick segue into Pattern 1 of the D minor pentatonic scale. (The transitional C and A notes at the top of measure 25 are part of Pattern 2 of D minor pentatonic.) A legato-fueled roller-coaster ride ensues with a scalar "climb/fall back/climb" lick that gains intensity with ever-escalating rhythms. (Note the brief stopover in the D minor pentatonic "lower extension box" [see Chapter 1].) Classic bending maneuvers (see Figs. 5A–C) provide the muscle in measures 29–30, and the section closes with a Pattern 2 phrase that culminates in an anticipatory quarter note triplet-driven scale ascension. Notice how this simple phrase creates a sense of expectation for things to come.

D Section (measures 33–40):

What "comes" is an ultra-smooth transition back to the A minor pentatonic scale, where a set of bends in the top portion of Pattern 4 herald the return to the key of A minor. A response phrase slips down Patterns 3 and 2, followed by a pattern-juggling phrase (inspired by Fig. 27D) that climbs back up the neck, and the solo goes out on a heavily vibratoed high-A note (bent from G on the high-E string) and a dyad slide (E/C) down the fretboard.

Tone Tips

Guitar: solidbody electric

Pickup Selection: bridge

Pickup Type: humbucker

Gain: 8

EQ: Bass/Middle/Treble: 3/10/6

Effects: heavy reverb (bright hall), moderate delay with long slap (approx. 450ms)

 TRACK 28

Fig. 28 "Solo 4A"

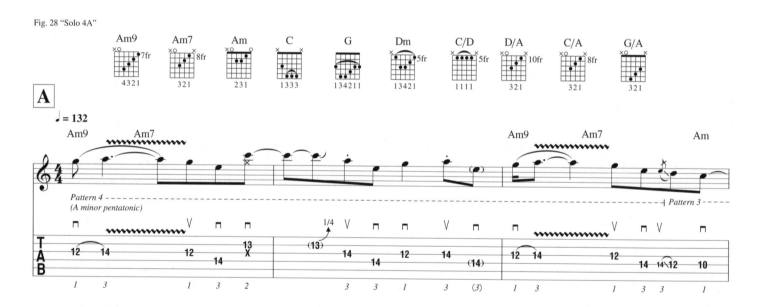

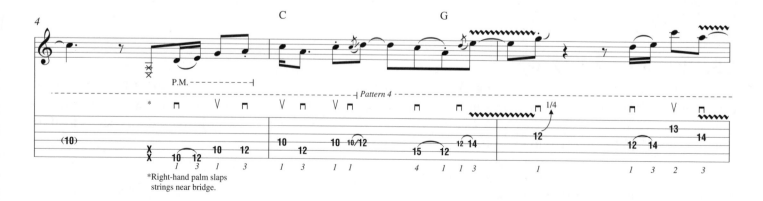

*Right-hand palm slaps strings near bridge.

Connecting Pentatonic Patterns

Solo 4B

Style: Uptempo Hard Rock
Scales/Patterns:
> A Minor Pentatonic: Patterns 1, 2, 3, and 4
> D Minor Pentatonic: Patterns 1, 2, 3, and 4

Skill Level: Intermediate/Advanced

The performance in Solo 4B [**Fig. 29**] is Solo 4A on steroids! Performed over the same progression, the deployment tactics are similar, but the speed and intensity factors are taken to the next level.

A Section (measures 1–8):

The solo kicks off with a flurry of notes in Pattern 4 and an intense, fixed-string bend inspired by the example in Fig. 26A. By comparison, this one sounds nastier (in a good way) due, in large part, to the overtones of the distortion setting (overdrive channel of the amplifier) and the pickup selection (bridge humbucker instead of neck single coil). A sequenced "groups of 3" lick (see Figs. 4A, 4B, and 4D) falls down the scale in measure 4 and is followed by a pair of Pattern 3 phrases, which are divided by two rapid *glissando* (or *gliss*) string slides. (Slide quickly down the A string and then up the low-E string.) Measure 7 hosts the last official lick of this section. Based on the maneuvers of the "ping-pong" lick in Fig. 27F, it zips back and forth down Patterns 3 and 4. Take this one very slowly at first, working out the picking directions carefully.

B Section (measures 9–16):

The pickup notes at the end of measure 8 kick off the first phrase of the B section. A bit unorthodox, this passage (ending on beat 2 of measure 10) is based on the "pentatonic chord" concepts brought forth in Fig. 27H. Notice that this phrase involves the sweep-picking technique explained in Fig. 27G. By comparison, measures 10 and 11 offer a brief respite before the fire-breathing legato run in measure 12. The fingering is the easy part (basically, it's a two-finger lick); the picking directions will require some refinement. Start with the suggestions above the tab staff, but feel free to craft them to your personal taste. Measure 13 hangs its hat on the upper slice of Pattern 4 before making its way back down again via the sequenced "note-jumping" pattern explained in Fig. 4F (Chapter 1). The section resolves in the "symmetrical box" portion of Pattern 3 (see Figs. 18A and 19A in Chapter 3).

C Section (measures 17–32):

As explained in Solo 4A, the C section modulates to the key of D minor. This time the solo corresponds by moving to Pattern 4 of the D minor pentatonic scale (located at the fifth fret). In the first lick (measure 17), a whole-step bend on the G string results in a colorful "passing tone" (note outside of the scale). The passing tone in this instance is E, which is the second degree of the D natural minor scale (refer to Quick Theory Tutorial #6). A gradual bend highlights the second phrase (measures 18–19), which is a nod to Jimmy Page's immortal solo opener in Led Zeppelin's "Stairway to Heaven." The next phrase flirts with the "symmetrical box" portion of Pattern 3 (third and fifth frets of the low three string set) before climbing back up Pattern 4 at the end of measure 20. Upon arrival, it blends with Pattern 1 of the A minor pentatonic scale to greet the key change (back to A minor). The highlight of this four-bar passage is the five-note melodic motif that runs its course along the top three string set of all four patterns.

In measure 24, a descending scale run spills into place on the root of the D minor pentatonic scale (Pattern 1, at the 10th fret) smack dab on the downbeat of measure 25, where the key change occurs. (This particular soloing strategy is referred to as "note targeting.") Measures 25–26 host a distinctive phrase on the lower four string set (low-E, A, D, and G strings) that is mimicked in measures 27–28, on the next string set (A, D, G, and B). (These are elements of the "call-and-response" tactics explained in Solos 2A and 2B.) The cycled phrasing in measures 29–30 is spawned from the "Hideaway Lick" (first encountered and explained in measure 16 of Solo 2A), and the hand-spreader in measure 31 is inspired by Randy Rhoads' legato style. This lick actually crosses the bounds of two Patterns: the 13th fret of the high-E string is from Pattern 2, the 17th fret is from Pattern 3, and the 15th fret of the B string is a linking note from both patterns (see Fig. 27I). A grace-note slide brings us up to the 20th fret of the high-E string, and the section closes in the nether regions of the fretboard (Patterns 4 and 3 of D minor pentatonic). These small fret areas make for tight quarters, especially for large hands. Try squeezing your hand together like you're trying to cup an egg in your palm. This will force your fretting fingers closer together, allowing you to navigate the compact area.

D Section (measures 33–40):

At measure 33, the C section's closing lick resolves to the "higher" A note of the low-E string (17th fret)—perfect timing for the key change back to A minor! (Technically, we are now in the "higher-octave" version of the "lower extension box" of Pattern 1 [see Fig. 7A, Chapter 1].) Next, a pair of *gliss* slides ensue (one down the A string, the other up the low-E string) and a Pattern 3 phrase spins out an intricate rhythmic motif (the C–D–C note passage at the end of measure 34), which is picked up by Pattern 4 (note the pattern jump) and carried out in call-and-response fashion across measures 35–36. Ignoring the rests, the rhythmic form of the motif is: eighth/16th/dotted eighth. Refusing to be outdone by anything that has gone down previously, the solo closes on a fret-burning, "groups of 6" sequence that cascades down Pattern 4 and spills

Tone Tips

Guitar: solidbody electric

Pickup Selection: bridge

Pickup Type: humbucker

Gain: 9

EQ: Bass/Middle/Treble: 3/10/6

Effects: heavy reverb (bright hall), moderate delay with long slap (approx. 450ms)

into Pattern 3. Similar in tactics to the example explained in Fig. 4E of Chapter 1, the lick is largely constructed from matching legato maneuvers along three-string groupings. Work out the first six-note shape until you have it down cold, and then move on to the others. However, don't overlook the "curtain closer"—a high-voiced triple stop (three-note chord shape) sent slithering down the neck.

 TRACK 29

Fig. 29 "Solo 4B"

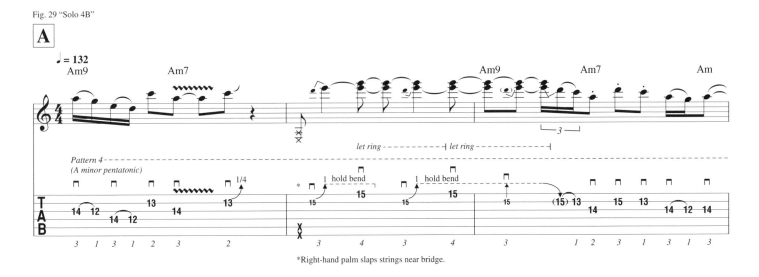

*Right-hand palm slaps strings near bridge.

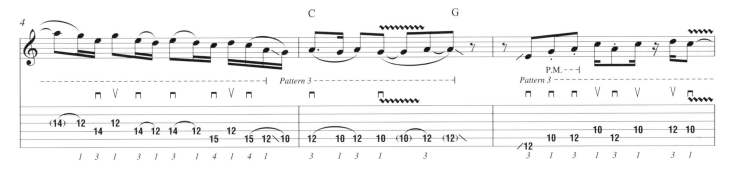

Connecting Pentatonic Patterns

Connecting Pentatonic Patterns

CHAPTER 5

PATTERN 5:
Putting It All Together

This chapter introduces Pattern 5, the final pentatonic pattern. Licks and connecting methods will be explored, as well as transposing techniques and concepts for soloing over the entire fretboard. As a bonus, this chapter includes four solos (instead of the usual two).

Pattern 5 of the A Minor Pentatonic Scale

Fig. 30A shows Pattern 5 of the A minor pentatonic scale. As in previous chapters, the top neck diagram depicts note placement, the middle diagram shows the note names, and the bottom one identifies the scale degrees. As you can see, there are three roots: the lowest root is on the low-E string, the "octave" root is on the G string, and the "highest" root is on the high-E string. Compared to the other patterns, Pattern 5 is the most symmetrical. The four-note box pattern on the lower string set (low-E and A strings) matches the one on the higher string set (B and high-E strings), while the middle string set (D and G strings) comprises an "elongated box" shape. Although the pattern is symmetrical, fret-hand fingering holds several options. As usual, the actual lick often dictates which fingering to use, so it's best to be prepared for any given situation. That said, **Fig. 30B** offers two sets of fingering suggestions. Practice running up and down the scale pattern, and experiment with those fingerings and other combinations.

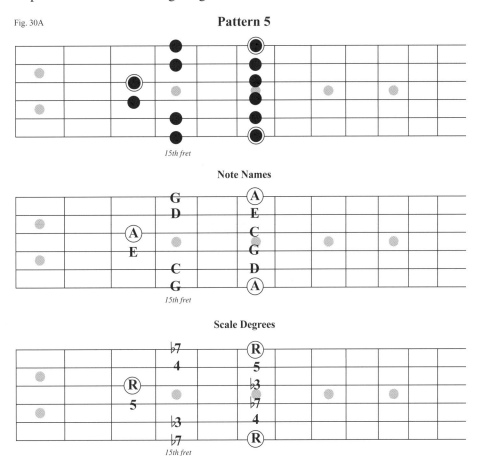

Fig. 30A **Pattern 5**

15th fret

Note Names

15th fret

Scale Degrees

15th fret

TRACK 30

Fig. 30B

Pattern 5 Licks

Many blues guitarists appreciate Pattern 5 for its string-bending faculties. **Fig. 31A** offers an example with a stock blues phrase that gives each ♭3rd (C) a quarter-step nudge (see Figs. 14A–D). Since this lick is voiced so high on the neck (where the frets are closer together), it's more comfortable to use the ring (3rd) finger on the 17th-fret notes, rather than the pinky.

TRACK 31
0:00

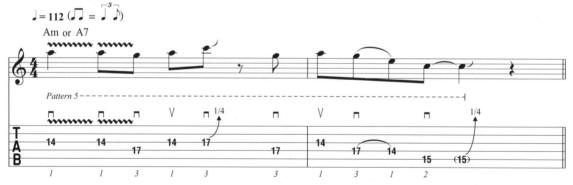

Fig. 31A (neck & bridge humbuckers; medium overdrive)

Fig. 31B is yet another example of the "Hideaway Lick" maneuver (refer to measure 16 of Solo 2A). This one involves the 4th, 5th, and ♭7th (D, E, and G) of the scale, making it equally useful for Am (A–C–E) and A7 (A–C♯–E–G) chords. Again, the ♭3rd (C) receives a bluesy quarter-step bend.

TRACK 31
0:09

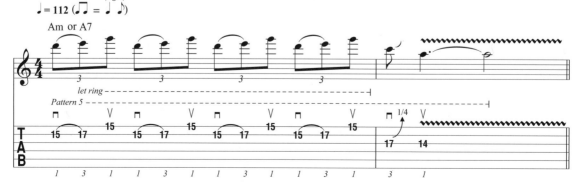

Fig. 31B (neck & bridge humbuckers; medium overdrive)

Fig. 31C executes the "Hideaway Lick" technique on the low string set, cycles it three times, and ends with a pair of double stops. Some rockers like to use these types of dyad figures as inverted power chord shapes (root on top, 5th on the bottom). Ritchie Blackmore's (Deep Purple) "Smoke on the Water" riff offers a prime example of inverted power chords.

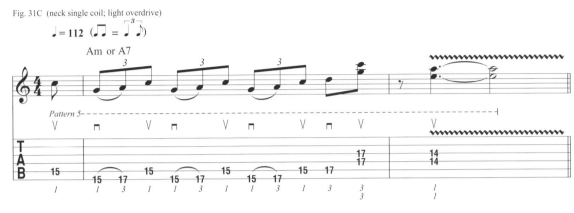

Fig. 31D tumbles down Pattern 5 in a three-string sequence of pull-off ploys. Based on the example in Fig. 4E (Chapter 1), it begins with a five-note sequence, effortlessly segues to a six-note pattern, and then resolves neatly to the root (A) on the G string.

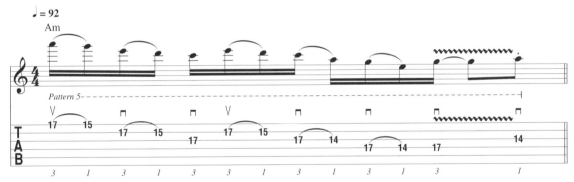

The pickup notes in **Fig. 31E** take full advantage of the symmetrical box shape on the middle strings. Be careful with the timing of this lick; it starts on the "and" of beat 3.

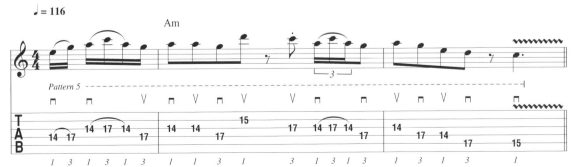

Fig. 31F slaps a little "Hendrix-ian" double-stop action on the upper portion of Pattern 5. This passage requires dead-on picking accuracy. Be careful so as not to strike any surrounding strings with the pick—it could result in some ugly-sounding notes!

TRACK 31
0:58

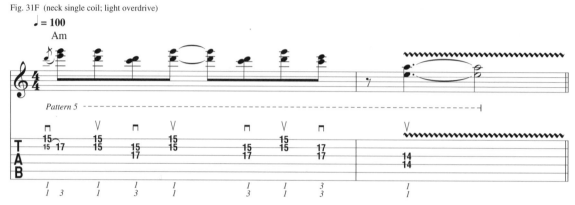

Fig. 31F (neck single coil; light overdrive)

Snapping in the Final Puzzle Piece

The top neck diagram in **Fig. 32A** on the next page illustrates how the five patterns of the A minor pentatonic scale "snap" into place along the fretboard. A large rectangle (heavy dark lines on top and bottom, squiggly lines on the sides) houses Patterns 1–5 along the neck, from Pattern 1 at the fifth fret to Pattern 5 at the 15th fret. (These are the patterns that we've been working with so far.) As you can see, Pattern 5 connects with Pattern 4 at the 14th and 15th frets. Pattern 5 ends at the 17th fret, but that leaves us with "leftover" frets (most electric guitars stretch to the 21st or 22nd fret). What to do? The answer is: we start over with Pattern 1.

Confused? Well, look at the fifth-fret notes of Pattern 1 in the second neck diagram. They are: A–D–G–C–E–A, low to high. Now look at the 17th-fret notes of Pattern 5. They're the same—only an octave higher. That's because the notes on the fretboard repeat themselves every 12 frets. As a result, the patterns repeat themselves, too. Look at the top neck diagram again. The "higher" notes on each string of Pattern 5 link with the "lower" notes of Pattern 1. The same goes for the fretboard area below Pattern 1 at the fifth fret. The "lower octave" location of Pattern 5 connects to Pattern 1. (Notice that the bottom four notes of Pattern 5 are the same exact notes as the "lower extension box" from Chapter 1.) There's even room left over below Pattern 5. This is where the "open position" form of Pattern 4 snaps into place. And there you have it: five patterns of the A minor pentatonic scale, all interconnecting along the fretboard!

Before we get to some lick examples, practice playing through all the patterns, connecting them along the neck. **Fig. 32B** offers a practice suggestion. The example starts by ascending the "open position" location of Pattern 4. At the top of the pattern it uses a "shift slide" (the fretting finger slides to a higher note on the same string, and the string is plucked upon its arrival) to segue to Pattern 5. Once the exercise returns to the low-E string, another shift slide takes you to Pattern 1, and you continue the process until topping off in the "upper octave" location of Pattern 1.

Fig. 32A

A Minor Pentatonic Patterns Along the Fretboard

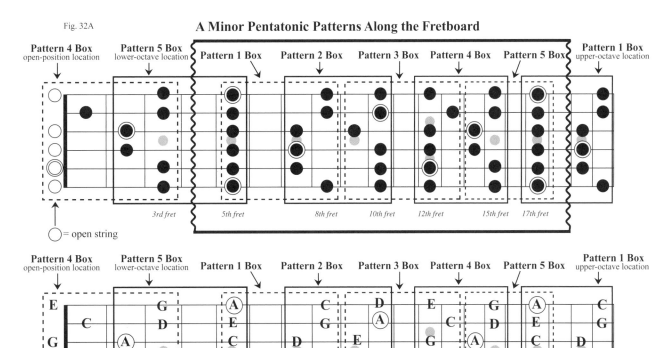

= open string

TRACK 32

Fig. 32B

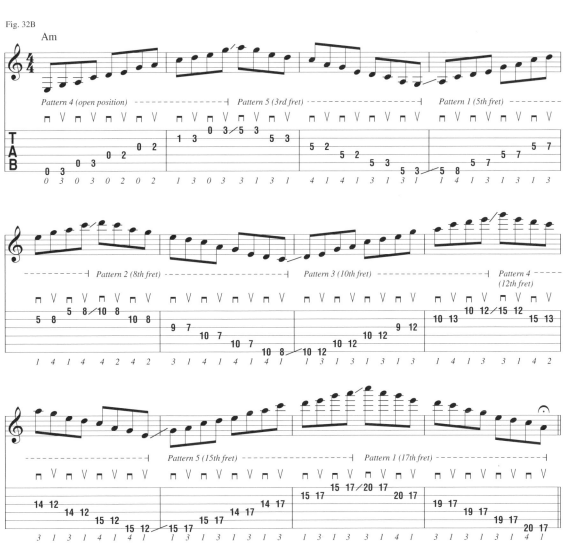

Connecting Pattern 5 to Its Upstairs and Downstairs Neighbors

Like savvy commuters, many guitarists often use Pattern 5 as a "secret corridor" to travel between their favorite Pattern 4 and Pattern 1 licks. **Fig. 33A** offers an example of this "routing" procedure. Measure 1 opens with an ascending phrase in the "upper octave" location of Pattern 1. At the top, a sliding-4ths dyad (see Fig. 10K, Chapter 1) segues down to Pattern 5 for a bluesy lick that connects with the Pattern 4 destination.

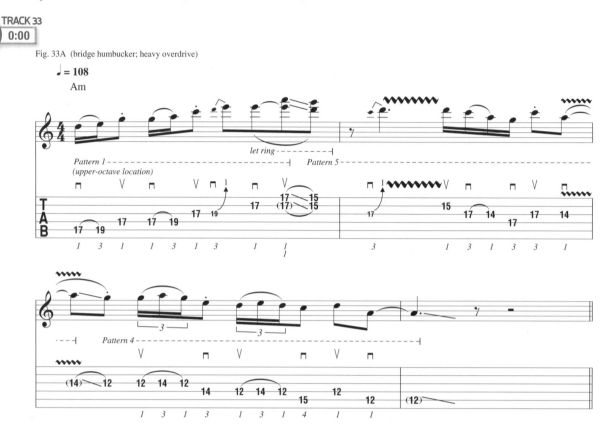

Fig. 33B travels in the opposite direction, starting with a sequenced phrase in Pattern 4, sliding up to Pattern 5 for a brief stopover, and then scooting up to a Pattern 1 (upper-octave location) resolution. (Note the inclusion of the inverted power chord dyads discussed in Fig. 31C.)

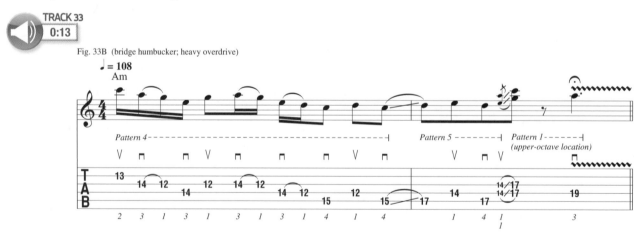

Fig. 33C focuses on the lower section of the fretboard with a meaty riff that travels downward from Pattern 1, across Pattern 5 (lower-octave location), and into Pattern 4 (open-position location). (Notice that Pattern 5 is being used in the same way the "lower extension box" was used in Chapter 1.) This example is kind of tricky, so take it very slowly. The first stumbling block occurs on the first beat, where a "double rollover" (refer to Figs. 4F–G in Chapter 1) is employed by the ring (3rd) finger. The other hurdle occurs in measure 2, where proper picking directions are of utmost importance.

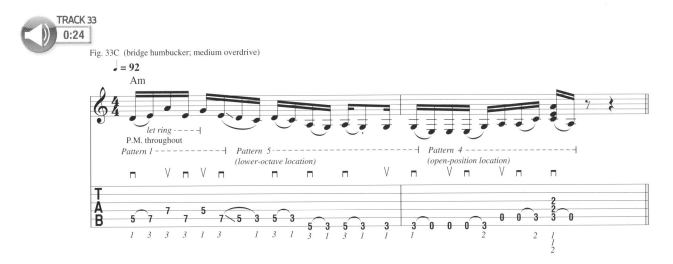

TRACK 33
0:24

Fig. 33C (bridge humbucker; medium overdrive)

Fig. 33D is a rip-roaring phrase perfectly suited for a southern rock boogie (uptempo shuffle). The passage starts in Pattern 1 with an ascending "hammer-on/adjacent-string" sequence (see Fig. 27E, Chapter 4) that tops off with a sliding-4ths dyad, which slips into the Pattern 5 saddle at the end of measure 2. Measure 3 features a rockabilly-style lick that incorporates notes from Pattern 4 (open position) and Pattern 5. (Jimmy Page used similar moves in his famed solo break in Led Zeppelin's "Heartbreaker.") The phrase goes out on an open-position A5 power chord voicing.

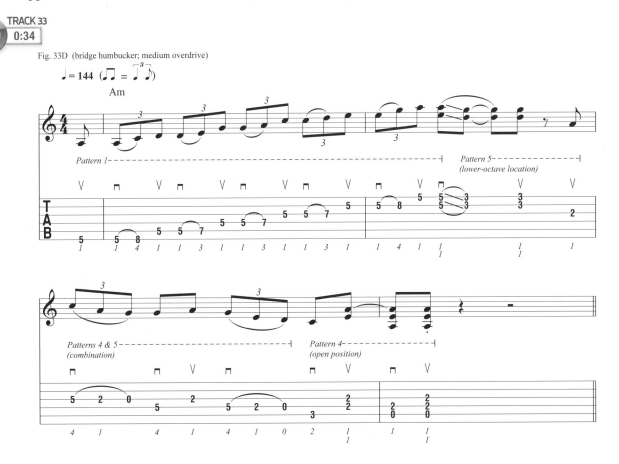

TRACK 33
0:34

Fig. 33D (bridge humbucker; medium overdrive)

Neck-Spanning Licks

The following six examples link all of the patterns together to form "neck-spanning" licks. In other words, extended licks that travel up or down a long section of the fretboard. The first one [Fig. 34A] is a grungy, riff-like example—the kind Neil Young might play. It starts with a collection of melodic double-stop maneuvers in the "open-position location" of Pattern 4, reinforced with an open high-E string "drone" (the string is allowed to ring, creating the aural illusion of another guitar playing rhythm). In measure 2, the lick moves up to Pattern 5 via a pinky-finger slide on the A string (be sure to use your pinky rather than your ring finger). Another pinky slide—this time, on the low-E string—shifts the phrase to Pattern 1, where another double-stop melody triggers an answering phrase in Patterns 2 and 3. Perhaps the most challenging aspect of this example is allowing some notes to ring together while employing counterpoint moves with other fretting fingers. If you follow the fingering suggestions and picking directions faithfully, you should be OK.

Connecting Pentatonic Patterns

TRACK 34
0:00

Fig. 34A (bridge & neck humbuckers; medium/heavy overdrive)

Fig. 34B covers the neck region from the 20th fret of the B string, all the way down to the third fret of the A string. The majority of the moves in each pattern have been featured, in one form or another, in previous licks in the book. So, put the example together, bar by bar, and then play it in its entirety when you have each pattern lick down cold.

TRACK 34
0:20

Fig. 34B (bridge humbucker; medium/heavy overdrive)

Fig. 34C is a bluesy example that snakes its way up the neck, slithering across every pattern in its path. Check out the tonal texture of that final "harmonic interval!" (See Quick Theory Tutorial #2, in Chapter 1.)

TRACK 34
0:33

Fig. 34C (bridge humbucker; medium/heavy overdrive)

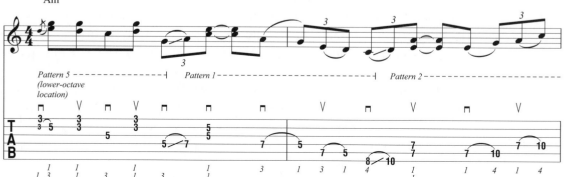

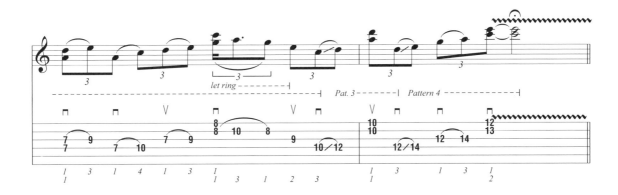

Discounting the 21st and 22nd frets, **Fig. 34D** leaves no section of the fretboard untouched! Starting out in the upper-octave location of Pattern 1, the phrase drops down the entire length of the neck via a set of adjacent-string sequences (the six-note patterns in measures 1 and 2) and a "groups of 3" sequence (measure 3 and 4).

TRACK 34
0:51

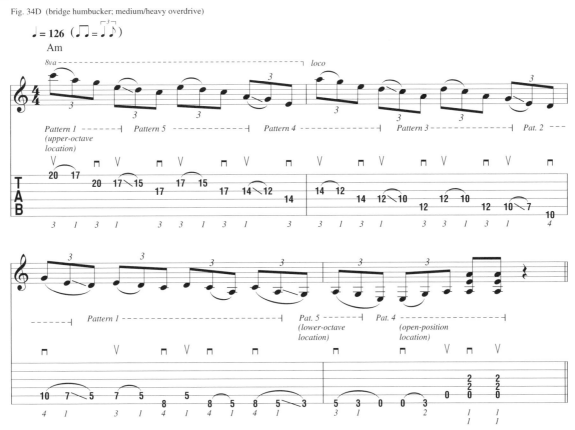

Fig. 34D (bridge humbucker; medium/heavy overdrive)

It's important to understand that long phrases, such as the previous two, can often be used in solos in a condensed fashion. For example, you could play the first measure of Fig. 34C and move on to another lick of your choosing. Or, one might choose to play only measure 3 of Fig. 34D and then skip to the A5 power chord rhythm that ends the phrase. The same goes for any of the licks and passages in this book. Memorize the ones you like best, and then craft them to your personal taste.

Fig. 34E travels the entire span of the neck by riding the top strings of each pattern. Once you establish the picking pattern and the fingering, you should be able to get this up to supersonic speeds!

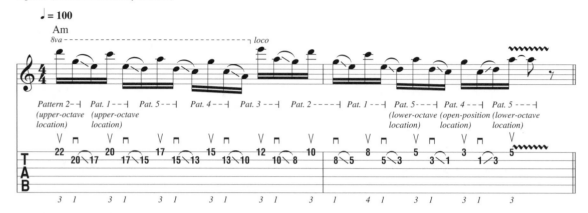

Fig. 34F is constructed from specific patterns that travel up the neck in three- and four-string bundles. Look closely and you'll find that the first measure establishes a three-string pattern that is repeated (an octave higher) in the second measure, legato moves and all. Measure 3 moves to a four-string pattern that is repeated (a 4th lower) in measure 4. Notice the identical legato moves.

Solo 5A

Style: Rock Shuffle
Scales/Patterns: A Minor Pentatonic: Patterns 1, 2, 4, and 5
Skill Level: Advanced Beginner/Intermediate

Solo 5A [**Fig. 35**] is an uptempo rock shuffle, or "boogie." Seventeen measures in length, it is entirely constructed from a cycled four-bar progression: one measure of A5 (A–E), one measure of C5 (C–G) to G5 (G–D), another measure of A5, and a final measure of C5 to D5 (D–A). (Refer to the chord frames at the top of the transcription.) It's interesting to note that all of the chords are diatonic to the A minor pentatonic scale (i.e., all notes are within the scale). Traditional theory aside, an analysis of the chord progression could read: I5–♭III5–♭VII5–I5–♭III5–IV5.

Measures 1–7:

The solo opens (pickup measure and measure 1) with a straightforward lick in Pattern 1, followed by a "sliding-4ths dyad" move (see Fig. 33A) that drops down to Pattern 5 (lower-octave location). Once situated, the phrase morphs into the "Hideaway Lick"(see Fig. 31B), segues to a brief "groups of 3" sequence (first half of measure 3), and then slips back up to Pattern 1 via a grace-note slide at the top of measure 4. Here, another straightforward lick (pull/hammer) ensues, followed by a major 3rd "harmonic interval" (see Quick Theory Tutorial #2 in Chapter 1) that is sent sliding down the fretboard. Measure 6 jumps back up to Pattern 1, where one "inverted power chord" slide maneuver (see Fig. 31C) inspires another in measure 7, which sends the phrase through Pattern 5, down into the open-position location of Pattern 4. The phrase officially ends on the open-A string note in measure 8. Take this two-measure passage very slowly at first. While not overly difficult, it's easy to overlook the intricacy of the rhythmic structure.

Measures 8–17:

The second half of the solo is a steady, incremental flight up the fretboard from open position to the "upper-octave location" of Pattern 5. The low-E string Pattern 4-to-Pattern 5 "hand-off" (see Figs. 33C and 34D) in measures 8–9 provides the launching pad for the first part of the journey. Inverted power chord dyads in measures 10–11 establish a theme that evolves into sliding 4ths in measure 12, but the official blast-off occurs in measure 13. Beginning here, each Pattern (1, 2, 4, and 5) provides a "stage" where top-string dyads are "targeted" as resting points to divide the rhythmic phrasing. (Listen to the audio to hear the motif in action.) Upon arrival at Pattern 5 (measure 15), dyads are withdrawn, but the motif accelerates with single-note targets (high D and E in measure 15, and high A in measure 16). When the top note is reached (17th fret of the high-E string), the solo goes out in a blaze of glory with a legato-fueled dive down the scale.

Tone Tips

Guitar: solidbody electric

Pickup Selection: bridge and middle

Pickup Type:
single coil (middle), humbucker (bridge)

Gain: 6

EQ: Bass/Middle/Treble: 6/4/4

Effects: moderate reverb (big room), moderate delay with short slap (approx. 150ms)

🔊 TRACK 35

Fig. 35 "Solo 5A"

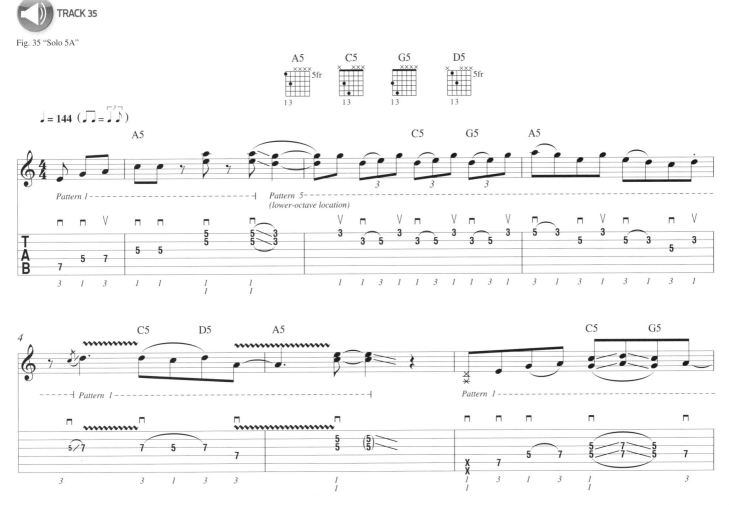

Connecting Pentatonic Patterns

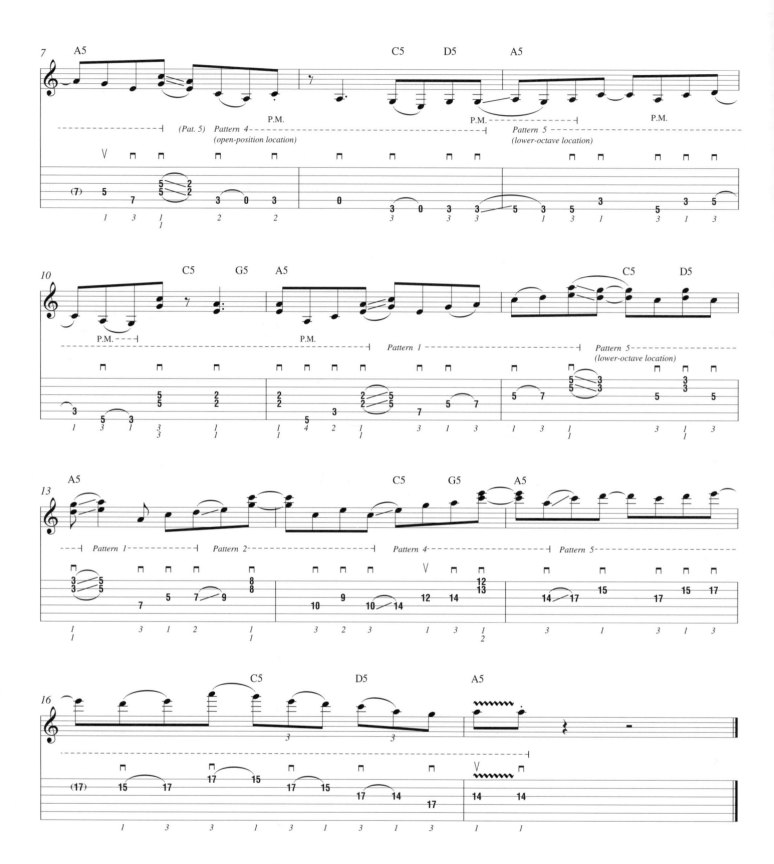

Solo 5B

Style: Rock Shuffle
Scales/Patterns: A Minor Pentatonic: Patterns 1, 2, 3, 4, and 5
Skill Level: Intermediate

Solo 5B [**Fig. 36**] is performed over the same progression and rhythm track as Solo 5A. While very similar in structure, the solo itself is more intense and requires more finesse and technique than its predecessor.

Measures 1–9:

The opening, a Pattern 1 lick (pickup measure and measure 1), is very similar to that of the previous solo (Fig. 35), except for the speedier entry (hammer-ons in the pickup measure). Again, the Pattern 5 "Hideaway Lick" is used in measure 2, but this time it is only performed once, moving instead to a set of hammer/pulls on the top two strings and a syncopated eighth-note phrase in measure 3. Be careful with the Jimmy Page-inspired "finger-spreader" lick in measure 4 (see Fig. 33D). This lick requires quite a bit of pinky strength for the pull-offs. Try dropping your fret-hand wrist toward the floor so you can get a better hand angle to work the necessary muscles. The end of measure 4 finds us in the open-position location of Pattern 4, where a string of A5 power chord grips are set against single-note pedal tones, played on the A and low-E strings. This sets up an interesting rhythm that is carried up into Pattern 5 (measure 6), where a pair of inverted power chord dyads (see Fig. 31C) are used as the catalysts to a neck-climbing lick that crosses the inner string sets of Patterns 1–4. This is the same type of approach that is explained in Fig. 34E; however, while that lick goes down the neck on the top two strings, this one ascends the A, D, and G strings and caps off with a quarter-step bend on the 13th fret of the B string (measure 9).

Measures 10–17:

An aggressive "fixed-string bend" lick (see Fig. 26A, Chapter 4) at the top of measure 10 kicks off a call-and-response phrase, which passes through measures 11–12. (Notice how the Pattern 4 melody in measure 11 is answered by the same melody, transposed down an octave in Pattern 3.) At the top of measure 13, a sneaky A-string slide (use your middle finger) triggers a super-legato phrase that takes full advantage of the symmetrical properties of Pattern 5 (refer to Fig. 30A). Just pick down on each adjacent string and let your fret-hand fingers do all the work! This phrase empties out into Pattern 1 (upper-octave location), where a bluesy bend precedes a rhythmically enhanced trip down the Patterns via the top two string set (see Fig. 34E), and the solo goes out on a "string-jumping" Pattern 3-to-Pattern 4 handoff (see Fig. 27E, Chapter 4).

Tone Tips

Guitar: solidbody electric

Pickup Selection: bridge and middle

Pickup Type:
single coil (middle), humbucker (bridge)

Gain: 6

EQ: Bass/Middle/Treble: 6/4/4

Effects: moderate reverb (big room),
moderate delay with short slap
(approx. 150ms)

 TRACK 36

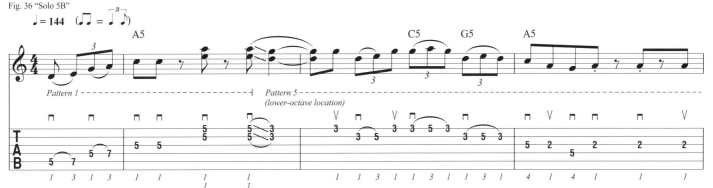

Fig. 36 "Solo 5B"

Connecting Pentatonic Patterns

Patterns 1–5 of the E Minor Pentatonic Scale

The neck diagrams in **Fig. 37A** illustrate how the five patterns of the E minor pentatonic scale (E–G–A–B–D) are aligned on the fretboard. (The top neck diagram shows the note placement; the bottom diagram identifies the actual note names.) These scale patterns fall in the exact same order as the A minor pentatonic scale patterns, except that the "primary" pattern, Pattern 1, is located in open position, and the "higher-octave location" of Pattern 1 is at the 12th fret. Keep in mind that the lowest E note on the fretboard is the open low-E string, putting it five frets (or five half steps) below A, which is at the fifth fret of the same string. It follows, then, that every note of the E minor pentatonic scale in this register is five frets below its A minor pentatonic counterpart. Therefore, each scale pattern (or position) of the E minor pentatonic scale is five frets below the matching pattern "number" of A minor pentatonic. Compare these neck diagrams to the ones in Fig. 32A and you should "get the picture." If you're still confused, you may want to refer back to Fig. 2 in Chapter 1.

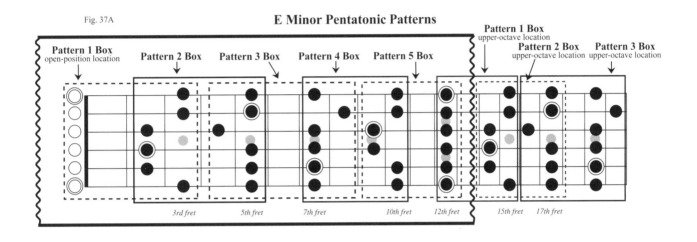

Fig. 37A   **E Minor Pentatonic Patterns**

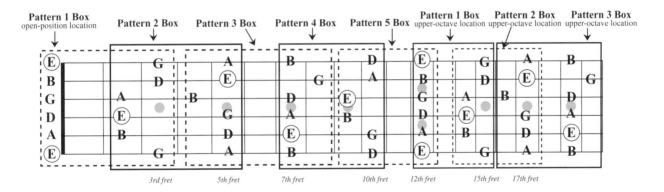

95

Connecting Pentatonic Patterns

We're going to forego lick examples and get right to an E minor pentatonic solo. Before we do, however, take some time to acquaint yourself with the E minor pentatonic "lay of the land" on the fretboard. **Fig. 37B** offers a practical exercise for adjusting yourself to the new key. Identical in approach to the example in Fig. 32B, it's designed to help you get started with connecting neighboring patterns of the E minor pentatonic scale along the fretboard.

 TRACK 37

Fig. 37B

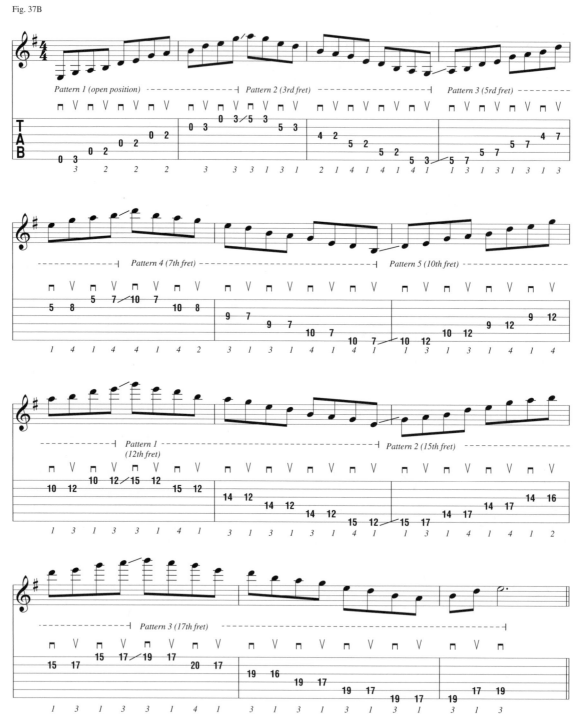

Solo 5C

Style: "Hip-Hop" Funk-Rock
Scales/Patterns: E Minor Pentatonic: Patterns 1, 2, 3, 4, and 5
Skill Level: Intermediate/Advanced

Solo 5C [**Fig. 38**] is performed over a funky E minor jam track. (See the chord frame at the top of the transcription for a suggested Em7 [E–G–B–D] chord voicing. Note: the 5th [B] is omitted from the voicing.) The "hip-hop" feel is courtesy of the "shuffled 16th-note" groove of the rhythm section. Shuffled 16ths mean the first and third 16th notes (in each one-beat grouping) receive the value of *two* notes of a 16th-note triplet, while the second and fourth 16th notes receive the value of *one*. Listen to the accompanying audio track for aural clarification. (For a complete breakdown of rhythmic notation, check out Chapter 2 of *Music Theory for Guitarists* [Hal Leonard].) The solo itself draws from every pattern of the E minor pentatonic scale (refer to Fig. 37A).

Measures 1–4:

The solo opens with a funky rendition of a Jimi Hendrix-inspired phrase (beats 1–3 of measure 1). Similar in structure to his often-copied "Hey Joe" opener, it combines Pattern 1 and 2 and includes an open high-E "drone" (refer to Fig. 34A). This is followed by a snarly open-position lick (beat 4 of measure 1 and beats 1–3 of measure 2) that ends on a subtle pinch harmonic (see Fig. 8B, Chapter 1) on the low-E string, and next comes another "Pattern 1 and Pattern 2 combination" lick. This one is sort of a reverse rendition of the Jimmy Page-type moves explained in Fig. 33D and measure 4 of Solo 5B (Fig. 36). The final phrase in this section (beat 4 of measure 3 and beats 1–3 of measure 4) is derived from the pattern-juggling examples from Figs. 27D–H in Chapter 4. The moves and the scale patterns (positions) are the same; it's just that they've been moved to a different part of the neck to align with E minor pentatonic. Before we move on, look back over the last four measures and notice the rhythmic "theme" of the section. The second, third, and fourth phrases begin with a "three 16th notes" pickup in the previous measure.

Measures 5–8:

Measures 5–6 witness further evidence of pattern-juggling tactics. Opening in the "symmetrical box" of Pattern 3 (see Figs. 19A–B), the first phrase momentarily slips into Pattern 4 before immediately falling back to Pattern 3. The next lick is a little trickier (measure 6). Beginning with a pull/hammer (E–D–E), it jumps to a passing open G string (all open strings are up for grabs in E minor pentatonic), zigzags along the D string (be sure to use the suggested fingering here), and ends on a couple of bluesy B-string bends. A grace-note slide on the high-E string initiates an intriguing Pattern 5 passage (measure 7). Fueled by a "16th-note/eighth-note" rhythmic motif, the phrase is constructed from wide intervallic jumps (6ths and 5ths) that are derived from the pattern itself. Aside from the initial jump (12th fret of the high-E string to the same fret of the G string), the rest of the sequence moves to lower adjacent strings. This section's capping lick hearkens all the way back to the Fig. 8A example in Chapter 1. Essentially, it's a "fancied-up" variation of the same lick, transported up the fretboard to align with the E minor pentatonic scale.

Measures 9–12:

The first phrase in this final section begins with pickup notes in measure 8. A "call-and-response" phrase of sorts, it begins with an ascending lick in Pattern 1 (upper-octave location), which is answered by a similarly contoured lick in Pattern 2 (upper-octave location). The "concluding" portion of the passage instigates a fiery phrase that races up Pattern 2. Based on a sequence we've seen before (see Fig. 9C, Chapter 1; Fig. 27E, Chapter 4; and Fig. 33D, Chapter 5), it involves a double pick attack on each string, followed by a hammer-on. (Be sure to follow the picking notation faithfully.) The closing phrases of the solo (end of measure 10 through measure 12) cover the longest section of the fretboard in the shortest amount of time (19th fret of the high-E string to the open low-E string). Measure 11 is directly related to the "string-bundling" method explained in Fig. 34F, while measure 12 is the low-string counterpart to the example explained in Fig. 34E.

Tone Tips

Guitar: solidbody electric

Pickup Selection: bridge

Pickup Type: humbucker

Gain: 7

EQ: Bass/Middle/Treble: 4/8/8

Effects: light reverb (small hall)

Connecting Pentatonic Patterns

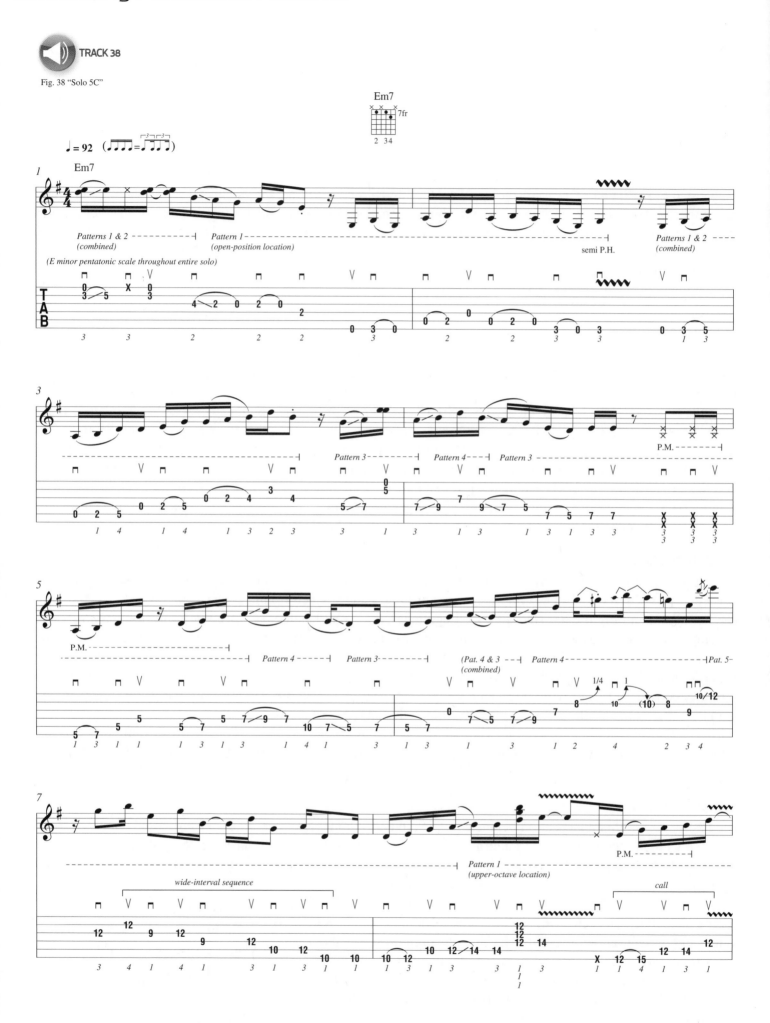

Patterns 1–5 of the B Minor Pentatonic Scale

The two neck diagrams in **Fig. 39A** illustrate how the five patterns of the B minor pentatonic scale (B–D–E–F#–A) are aligned on the fretboard. Again, they fall in the same order as the A minor and E minor pentatonic scale patterns, except that the "primary" pattern, Pattern 1, is located at the seventh fret. (Note: there is no "open-position location" scale pattern for B minor pentatonic.) **Fig. 39B** offers a practice example for "burning in" the pattern connections in this new key.

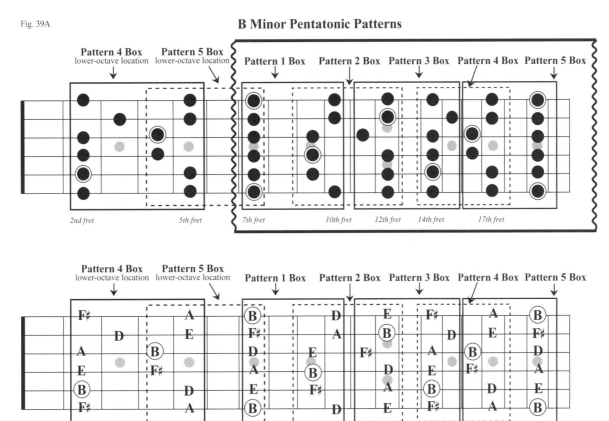

TRACK 39

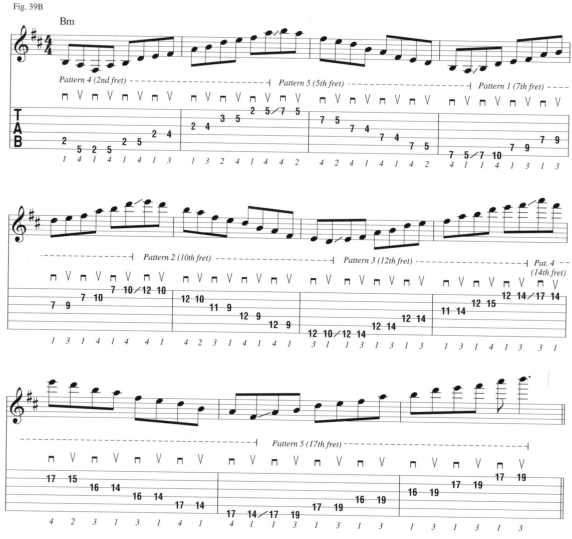

Solo 5D

Style: 12/8 Minor Blues Ballad
Scales/Patterns:
     B Minor Pentatonic: Patterns 1, 2, 3, 4, and 5
     E Minor Pentatonic: Patterns 1, 2, 3, 4, and 5
     F# Minor Pentatonic: Pattern 1
Skill Level: Intermediate/Advanced

Solo 5D [**Fig. 40**] is based on a 12-bar blues progression in the key of B minor. Constructed from the i, iv, and v chords (Bm7, Em7, and F#m7) of the B minor scale (B–C#–D–E–F#–G–A), the form is as follows: Bm7 (four bars), Em7 (two bars), Bm7 (two bars), F#m7 (one bar), Em7 (one bar), Bm7–Em7 (three bars), Bm7 (*cadenza* ending). Throughout the solo, corresponding minor pentatonic scales are used for each chord change. In other words, the B minor pentatonic scale is used over the Bm7 chords, the E minor pentatonic scale is used for the Em7 chords, and the F# minor pentatonic scale (F#–A–B–C#–E) services the solitary F#m7 chord (measure 9). The groove is a very slow shuffle—ballad style. The 12/8 notation allows for clearer comprehension of the rhythms involved. Hint: try to "feel" the meter as standard 4/4 time, with eighth-note triplets occupying each beat. A good method for counting in 12/8 is: "one-and-uh, two-and-uh, three-and-uh, four-and-uh."

Measures 1–4:

The solo starts with a pickup phrase in Pattern 1 of the B minor pentatonic scale. (Using the aforementioned counting method, the phrase starts on the "uh" of beat 3.) Note-wise, this is just another of the innumerable variations on the classic phrase in Fig. 5A of Chapter 1. Whereas that one is in A minor, this one is two frets higher, in the key of B minor. The second phrase enters in the same section of measure 1 ("uh" of beat 3). Rhythmically, this phrase establishes an eighth-note theme interspersed with 16th-note "jabs." Moving up to Pattern 2, the third phrase ("and" of beat 3 in measure 2 through measure 3) picks up on the rhythmic theme, but like a crafty boxer, delays the jabs until the end of the phrase. The last lick of this section (measure 4) walks down Pattern 2, spills into Pattern 1, and drops down to the "lower-octave location" of Pattern 5. Structurally, this phrase is very similar to the step-by-step process originally explained in Fig. 9G of Chapter 1.

Measures 5–10:

Measure 5 brings the iv chord change (Em7), and the solo shifts to E minor pentatonic. The phrasing starts in Pattern 1 (open-position location), with a "chord-change establishing" open low-E string attack followed by a trill on the D string. For the trill, attack the open D string and rapidly cycle a series of hammer/pulls to and from the second fret of the same string. Measure 6 kicks off with a "Pattern 1-and-Pattern 2 combination" lick (refer to measures 1–4 of Solo 5C), followed closely by a crafty two-finger dyad shape (middle finger on the fourth fret of the G string; index finger on the third fret of the B string) that is launched in Pattern 2, slid up to Pattern 4, and, just at the perfect moment (the downbeat of measure 7), nestles into the 10th- and 11th-fret area of Pattern 2 of the B minor pentatonic scale. Here, it sits for a full measure while the two notes are attacked separately with a cycled rhythm pattern. Fret-hand vibrato intensifies this emotional passage. At the top of measure 8, a descending lick breaks the repetition, spilling from Pattern 2 down into Pattern 1. (This lick has its origins in the example explained in Fig. 9B of Chapter 1.) A slow slide on the A string bypasses Pattern 2, settles briefly into Pattern 3, and finishes off with a sequenced phrase in Pattern 4.

Measure 9 heralds the v (F♯m7) chord, and the solo segues seamlessly to the closest pattern available for the F♯ minor pentatonic scale (F♯–A–B–C♯–E). How convenient—it just so happens that Pattern 1 (upper-octave location) occupies the same fretboard territory as the previous lick! (See the neck diagram above measure 9 of the transcription.) Taking full advantage of this overlapping phenomenon, the phrase starts with a "common tone" (a note that belongs to both scales) whole-step bend from the 17th fret of the B string. Not to appear overly calculated or pretentious, the phrase itself goes for emotion rather than excessive technique. (The lick is a hybrid of Figs. 5A–B from Chapter 1.) At measure 10, it's back to the iv (Em7) chord and the phrasing slips right into Pattern 2 (upper-octave location) of the E minor pentatonic scale with a brawny Stevie Ray Vaughan-style double-stop bend (refer to Fig. 14E for technical advice). At mid-measure, a pair of string *glisses* ensue (rapid, extended slides), and the measure goes out on a Pattern 1-to-Pattern 5 "handoff" phrase.

The "Outro":

Normally, in a 12-bar blues, measure 11 starts the "turnaround" chord cadence (see "Measures 1–12" analysis in Solo 2A, Chapter 2). In this performance, measure 11 begins an "outro" section, where the i and iv (Bm7 and Em7) chords are repeated until the end of the piece. In direct correlation to the chords, the solo also pivots from the B minor pentatonic scale to the E minor pentatonic scale. As you work your way through this closing section, notice how the modulations (segues to different keys) are crafted so as to not sound "jumpy." For example, the measure 11 transition from B minor pentatonic to E minor pentatonic is only two frets below the last note of the B minor pentatonic phrase, and the modulation from measure 11 to measure 12 uses the overlapping scale pattern approach, as does the mid-measure changeover in measures 12 and 13.

Tone Tips

Guitar: solidbody electric

Pickup Selection: neck

Pickup Type: single coil

Gain: 7

EQ: Bass/Middle/Treble: 5/5/8

Effects: moderate reverb (large hall), moderate delay with short slap (approx. 200ms)

Connecting Pentatonic Patterns

TRACK 40

Fig. 40 "Solo 5D"

Connecting Pentatonic Patterns

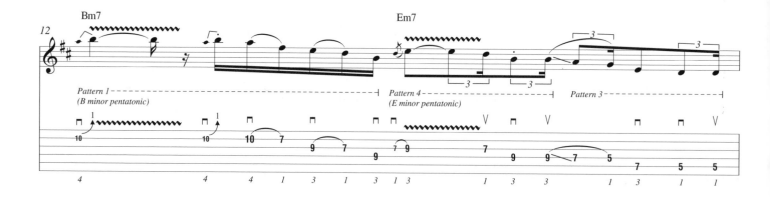

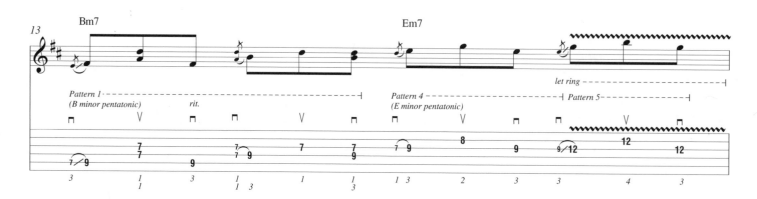

CHAPTER 6

MAJOR PENTATONIC PATTERNS

This chapter serves as a brief overview of the major pentatonic scale (1–2–3–5–6). Included are an explanation of the five patterns and how they link together, lick examples, tips for using the relative minor pentatonic scale as a "lick source," and three complete solos.

The Relative C Major Pentatonic Scale: Patterns 1–5

The minor pentatonic scale may be the "King Daddy" of rock, but the major pentatonic scale is a strong contender. Need evidence? Well, here's a short list of well-known rock solos that are based on the major pentatonic scale: "Let It Be" and "Get Back" by the Beatles, "Honky Tonk Women" and "Tumbling Dice" by the Rolling Stones, "Ramblin' Man" and "Jessica" by the Allman Brothers Band, "The Wind Cries Mary" and "May This Be Love" by the Jimi Hendrix Experience, "D'Yer Mak'er" and "Black Dog" by Led Zeppelin, "Lights" by Journey, "Take It Easy" by Eagles, "Rock This Town" by the Stray Cats, "Crazy Little Thing Called Love" by Queen, "Give Me Three Steps" by Lynyrd Skynyrd, and "The Golden Road" by the Grateful Dead. While this list features a diverse group of players, tones, and song styles, there is a common thread: all of the songs are based on major chords (root–3–5) and major scale chord progressions.

It may seem disheartening to think that you have to learn a whole new batch of scale patterns to tackle major pentatonic soloing. The truth is, if you've worked through the first five chapters of this book, you already know them! Quick Theory Tutorial #7 explains how the C major pentatonic scale is derived from the C major scale. The C major scale is "relative" (contains the same notes) to the A minor scale—*and* the A minor pentatonic scale is derived from the A minor scale (refer to Quick Theory Tutorial #1, Chapter 1). Do you see where we're going with this? Yes, the C major pentatonic scale (C–D–E–G–A) is relative to the A minor pentatonic scale (A–C–D–E–G). In other words, they share the same notes. That also means that they share the same scale patterns!

Quick Theory Tutorial #7

Like the minor pentatonic scale is to the natural minor scale (refer to Quick Theory Tutorial #1, Chapter 1), the *major pentatonic scale* is an abridged version of the *major scale*. Whereas the major scale contains seven notes, the major pentatonic scale contains five. For example, the C major scale is: C–D–E–F–G–A–B. The C major pentatonic scale omits the fourth and seventh scale tones, F and B, resulting in a five-note scale: C–D–E–G–A (1–2–3–5–6). Theoretically, this two-note exclusion omits the "awkward" half-step intervals (the space of one fret) between the 3rd and 4th and the 7th and tonic scale tones. On the fretboard, this translates to "finger-friendly" two-notes-per-string scale patterns.

Connecting Pentatonic Patterns

Take a look at **Fig. 41A**. The neck diagrams show the five patterns of the C major pentatonic scale and how they align on the fretboard. As with the minor pentatonic scale, the numbering system is based on the location of the roots: Pattern 1 has the roots on the low-E, D, and high-E strings; Pattern 2 has its roots on the D and B strings; the roots in Pattern 3 are on the A and B strings; in Pattern 4, they are on the A and G strings; and the roots in Pattern 5 are on the low–E, G, and high-E strings. Compare these diagrams to the A minor pentatonic diagrams in Fig. 32A (Chapter 5) and you'll see that, although the roots and the pattern numbers differ, the box patterns themselves are identical.

Fig. 41A   **C Major Pentatonic Patterns Along the Fretboard**

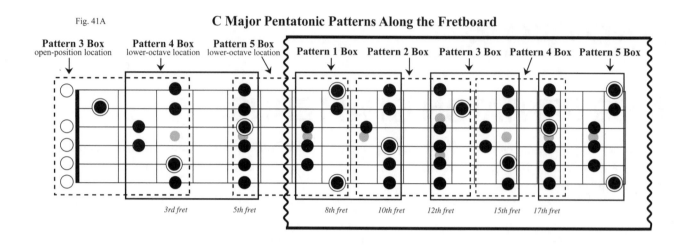

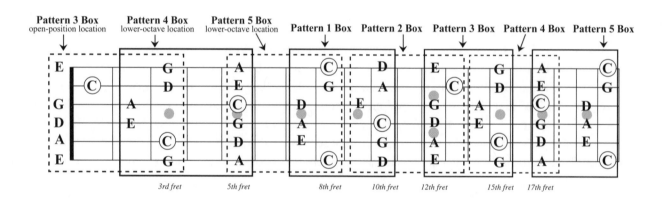

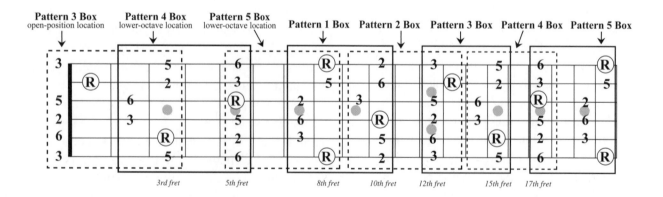

Of course, it isn't quite that simple. In order to use these "identical" major pentatonic patterns effectively, you'll need to feature, or emphasize, different notes—ideally, the root (C), 3rd (E), and 5th (G) of the scale. (The root, 3rd, and 5th form the tonic "triad construction," which can be considered the "heart" of the scale.) **Fig. 41B** is an exercise designed with this purpose in mind. The first phrase (Pattern 3, open-position location) is a simple melody that starts on the root (C), ascends to the 5th (G), backs off to the 3rd (E), and ascends to the octave root (C). Measure 3 jumps up to Pattern 4 (lower-octave location). This is essentially the same phrase, played in reverse fashion, again bringing out the true sound of the scale itself. The rest of the example continues with the same process, jumping from pattern to pattern, until capping off at the top of the fretboard. It's a great way to practice musically while getting a feel for the major pentatonic scale patterns.

TRACK 41

Fig. 41B

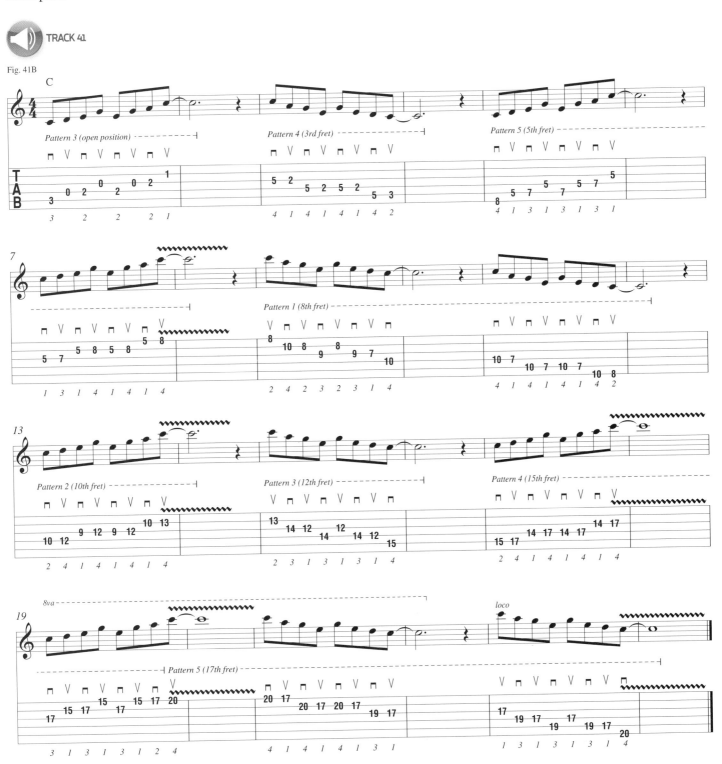

"Re-Crafting" Minor Pentatonic Licks

Now let's take a look at some major pentatonic lick examples that borrow from the relative A minor pentatonic licks found throughout this book. **Fig. 42A** is straight out of the Allman Brothers playbook. Crafted from Pattern 5 (lower-octave location), this lick has its origins in the examples from Figs. 3B–C, 5A, and 5C (Chapter 1). In this example, though, the notes of the C major triad are emphasized: the lick starts and ends on C (root), the sustained notes in measures 1 and 2 are G (5th) and E (3rd), and the bend targets an E note (3rd).

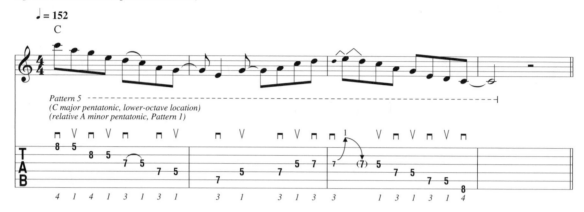

Fig. 42A (neck humbucker; light/medium overdrive)

Fig. 42B is a classic country bluegrass lick. Here, extra emphasis is placed on the root note (C), with two "bend targets," again hitting the 3rd (E).

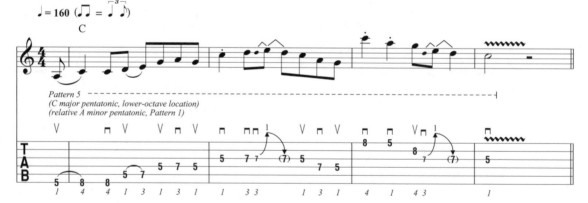

Fig. 42B (bridge single coil; very light overdrive)

Fig. 42C "re-crafts" the A minor pentatonic "Hendrix" examples in Figs. 6A–D of Chapter 1, retrofitting them for a C major harmony. Take notice of the featured dyad in the first measure (C/G = root and 5th) and the starting and ending couplets in measure 2 (C/E = 3rd and root; G/E = 5th and 3rd). These dyads fortify the phrase with a distinct C major tonality. Just as Pattern 1 of the minor pentatonic scale is a favorite of many rock and blues soloists, so, too, is Pattern 5 of the major pentatonic scale. This stands to reason, as both scale patterns are virtually identical, except that the roots are in different locations.

TRACK 42
0:20

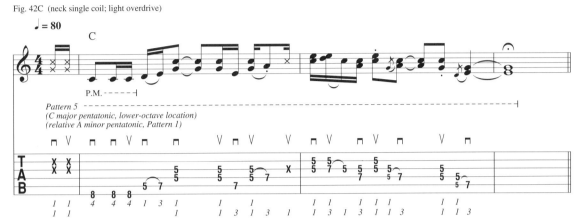

Fig. 42D is a rockabilly example, the kind of lick Scotty Moore (Elvis Presley), James Burton (Ricky Nelson and Elvis Presley), Danny Cedrone (Bill Haley), Cliff Gallup (Gene Vincent), Brian Setzer (Stray Cats), or even Brian May (Queen's "Crazy Little Thing Called Love") might play. Note the "Hideaway Lick" (see Fig. 16 [measure 16]) at the end of measure 1, the fancy bend/release/pull (see Fig. 11 [measure 2] and Fig. 14F) in measure 2, and the C6 chord voicing (see the "chord-crafting" explanation in Fig. 27H) that caps off the lick.

TRACK 42
0:35

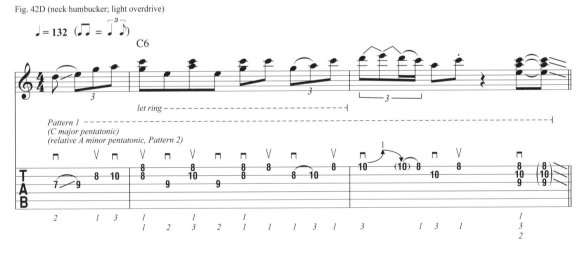

Connecting Pentatonic Patterns

Fig. 42E serves up a smorgasbord of the legato techniques demonstrated throughout this book. The blistering example manages to hit every pattern of the C major pentatonic scale as it makes mincemeat of a long section of the fretboard (from the 15th fret of the high-E to the third fret of the low-E string). Take your time with this one, as it contains calculated picking directions and fingerings. Watch out for those "pattern combination" passages in measures 2 and 5, as they require a wide reach with the fretting hand (see Fig. 29 [measures 31–32]).

TRACK 42
0:44

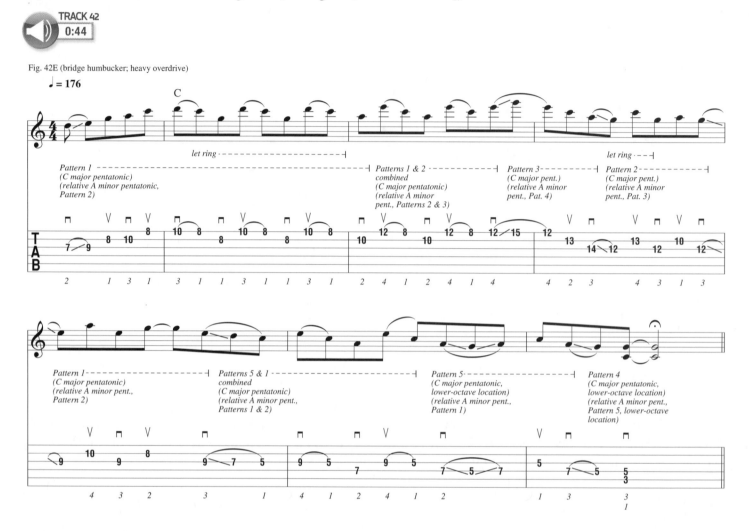

Fig. 42E (bridge humbucker; heavy overdrive)

Fig. 42F is a riff-like passage inspired by the soul/R&B stylings of Steve Cropper (Booker T. & the M.G.'s, Otis Redding, and the Blues Brothers). Essentially, an assortment of double-stop maneuvers interspersed with single-note passages, it runs from open position (Pattern 3) to the eighth fret (Pattern 1). Play this in a percussive fashion, using fret-hand palm-muting (see Fig. 3D, Chapter 1) to dampen the notes.

TRACK 42
1:24

Fig. 42F (bridge single coil; very light overdrive)

Solo 6A

Style: "Stones" Groove
Scales/Patterns: C Major Pentatonic: Patterns 1, 2, 3, 4, and 5
Skill Level: Beginner/Intermediate

Our first major pentatonic solo [**Fig. 43**] is influenced by the classic Rolling Stones teamwork of Keith Richards and Mick Taylor (early '70s). Based on the I, IV, and V chords (C, F, and G) of the C major scale (see Quick Theory Tutorial #8 below), the progression is similar in structure to the 12-bar blues progression in Solos 2A and 2B. But where that progression uses all dominant seventh chords, this one uses basic major triad chords (root–3rd–5th). The groove is medium rock, and the entire solo is constructed from the C major pentatonic scale.

Measures 1–7:

The solo opens with a pair of phrases carved from Pattern 5 (lower-octave location). The first (measure 1) is a variation on the fundamental minor pentatonic example in Fig. 5A. (To help you understand the correlation, the transcription includes the relative A minor pentatonic pattern numbers below each C major pentatonic pattern.) The second phrase (measures 2–3) features two bending techniques that we've encountered before. The first is a classic "Stones" maneuver: the repeated attack on a pre-bent note; in this case, a whole-step bend on the B string. (This procedure was first encountered in measure 23 of Solo 4A, Chapter 4.) The second is the "fixed-string bend" in measure 3. (This technique was explained in the "pedal steel" lick in Fig. 19G, Chapter 3.) Measure 4 begins a handoff phrase that drops down into Pattern 4 (lower-octave location). This phrase (measures 4–5) contains elements of the "ping-pong" lick in Fig. 27F, Chapter 4. At measure 6, it's back to Pattern 5 for a two-bar phrase that's not unlike the bluegrass lick from Fig. 42B.

Measures 8–16:

Measure 8 hosts the pickup notes of a two-bar phrase that spans measures 9 and 10. Fashioned from the top three strings of Pattern 1, it's basically a stripped-down (and decelerated!) version of the rockabilly lick from Fig. 42D. Spilling back down to Pattern 5 in measure 11, the solo then makes a jump to Pattern 2 at the top of measure 12. This sets off a "two-16ths/eighth-note" rhythmic motif (see Solo 3A [measure 4], Chapter 3) that propels the phrase up Pattern 2 and into Pattern 3 at the juncture of measures 12 and 13. This leads to another "Stones" trademark phrase in measure 13: a slow-moving, fixed-string bend on the top string set (high-E and B strings). This move is very similar in structure to the bluesy example in Fig. 26A, Chapter 4. Finally, the solo goes out on a gradually descending passage that makes its way down Pattern 3, skids across Pattern 2, and nestles into the lower pocket of Pattern 1.

Quick Theory Tutorial #8

Major scale harmony refers to the process of putting specific scale tones together to create chords (see Quick Theory Tutorial #5, Chapter 3). For example, the C major scale is: C–D–E–F–G–A–B. In scale formula terminology, it reads: 1–2–3–4–5–6–7. Grouping the first, third, and fifth tones (in other words, every other note) of the scale creates a C major chord (C–E–G). This is called the triad harmony of the I (pronounced "one") chord. Adding the seventh tone of the scale (B) to the triad results in a Cmaj7 chord (C–E–G–B). This is the seventh chord harmony of the root of the scale and is symbolized as "Imaj7." Applying this process to each scale degree results in the following triads: C–Dm–Em–F–G–Am–B°. In Roman numeral terminology, this reads: I–ii–iii–IV–V–vi–vii°. The seventh chord harmony of the C major scale is: Cmaj7–Dm7–Em7–Fmaj7–G7–Am7–Bm7♭5. And in Roman numerals: Imaj7–iim7–iiim7–IVmaj7–V7–vim7–vii°7. (For an in-depth study of scale harmony, refer to the suggested companion book *Music Theory for Guitarists: Everything You Ever Wanted to Know but Were Afraid to Ask* [Hal Leonard].)

Tone Tips

Guitar: solidbody electric
Pickup Selection: bridge and neck
Pickup Type: single coils
Gain: 5
EQ: Bass/Middle/Treble: 5/6/7
Effects: moderate reverb (big room)

Connecting Pentatonic Patterns

TRACK 43

Fig. 43 "Solo 6A"

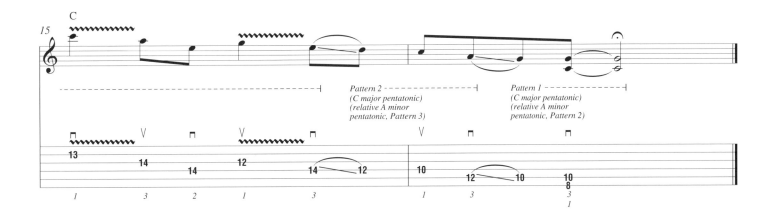

Solo 6B

Style: Uptempo "Arena" Rock
Scales/Patterns: C Major Pentatonic: Patterns 1, 2, 3, 4, and 5
Skill Level: Intermediate/Advanced

Solo 6B [**Fig. 44**] is, essentially, a rocking romp over a I–IV (C–F) progression in the key of C (see Quick Theory Tutorial #8). The C/E chord is simply an "inversion" of the C chord. *Inversion* means that a chord tone other than the root is voiced on the bottom of the chord. Here, the 3rd of the chord (E) is in the bass, fortifying the major tonality of the progression. Taking this into account, the progression follows a four-bar pattern that consists of two bars of I (C) and two bars of IV (F). The four-bar pattern is cycled four times (measures 1–16), and the solo goes out over a sustained C chord (measures 17–19). The groove and style is similar to the "arena rock" bands of the '70s and '80s, such as Journey, Boston, Van Halen, KISS, Foreigner, and .38 Special.

The Buildup and Big Tease:
Seventy-five percent of the solo (pickup measure and bars 1–14) is an anticipatory overture of what will evolve into the fiery finish. In other words, the soloist is teasing the audience with "glimpses" of the impending, explosive climax. For instance, the legato flurry in the pickup measure (Pattern 5, lower-octave location) immediately eases off into a pair of slow, melodic phrases in measures 1–3. Measures 4–7 continue with a "singable" melodic theme, but tucked between the easy-going lines are 16th-note embellishments, which spark the phrases with added energy. Not to mention, from a visual standpoint, pattern-juggling licks (see Figs. 20B–F, Chapter 3) such as these can really captivate an audience! In measure 8, a triplet-fueled phrase momentarily stirs up the troops, but, as if to say, "Not quite yet," measure 9 eases off into a pair of sustained, inverted power chord dyads (see Fig. 31C, Chapter 5). In measure 10, the momentum picks up in earnest with a speedy Pattern 5-to-Pattern 4 handoff lick (see Figs. 8D–F, Chapter 1, and measures 7–8 of Fig. 17, Chapter 2). This kicks off a gradually ascending passage (measures 11–12) that peaks with a "Hideaway Lick"-inspired phrase (see Fig. 42D) in measure 13. A powerful "two-16ths/quarter-note" rhythmic motif (see measures 12–14 of Fig. 11, Chapter 1) is the driving force behind this captivating three-bar passage.

The Payoff and Cadenza:
In measure 14, the "Hideaway Lick" tease of the previous measure explodes into full-fledged 16th-note glory! In measure 15, this cycled three-note lick directly reverses itself, seamlessly morphing into a pull-off on the high-E string (rather than the B-string hammer-on), with the pedal-tone note on the B string (rather than high E). The solo peaks in measure 16 with a pattern-crossing variation of measure 15. Here, the 12th fret of the high-E string becomes the top note while the other two notes stay situated (see Fig. 42E). This three-measure section (14–16) is a particularly demanding passage that requires deft picking accuracy and staunch legato techniques. Practice each measure separately (and slowly) before putting them all together.

Connecting Pentatonic Patterns

The closing section of the solo (measures 17–19) contains the *fermata cadenza*. That's a term used in traditional music theory. For the general music lover, a clearer description might be: the "show-off guitar ending!" It's where the band holds the last chord while the guitarist goes crazy, playing an array of fancy licks in "free time" (no specific tempo). This particular cadenza is based entirely on a collection of strategically placed scale sequence licks (see Figs. 4D–E, Chapter 1). In measure 17, a "groups of 4" lick segues to a pair of "groups of 5" segments, which spill into measure 18. A "groups of 3" insertion follows, and the cadenza goes out on another pair of "groups of 5" licks. These sequence segments may seem "willy-nilly," but there is a strategy behind the craftsmanship: look back over the passage and notice that each segue (with the exception of the "groups of 3" phrase) involves a "handoff" to the adjacent, higher string. If you follow the picking directions faithfully, you should have this entire passage up to speed in no time.

Tone Tips

Guitar: solidbody electric

Pickup Selection: neck

Pickup Type: humbucker

Gain: 5

EQ: Bass/Middle/Treble: 3/10/7

Effects: liberal reverb (bright hall), liberal delay with long slap (approx. 430ms)

TRACK 44

Fig. 44 "Solo 6B"

114

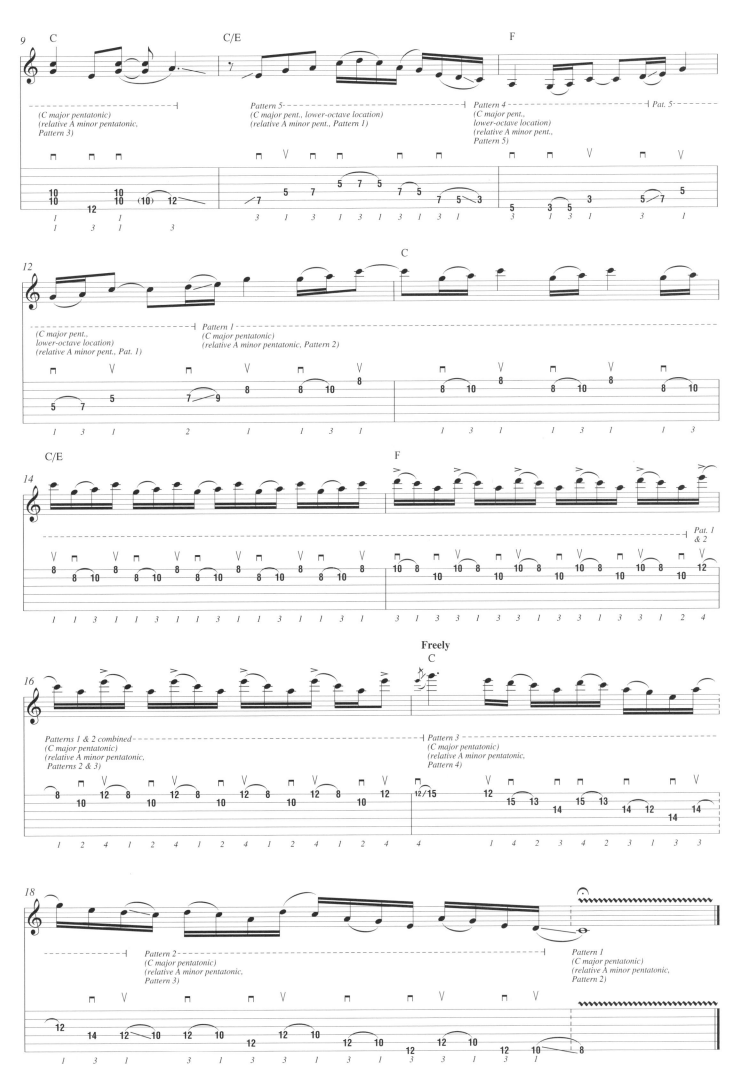

The G Major and D Major Pentatonic Scales

The upcoming solo (Solo 6C) poses a bit of a challenge, as it draws from three different scales: G major pentatonic (G–A–B–D–E), C major pentatonic (C–D–E–G–A), and D major pentatonic (D–E–F#–A–B). In preparation, the following figures outline the two scales that we haven't discussed: G major pentatonic and D major pentatonic.

Fig. 45A shows the five patterns of the G major pentatonic scale and how they connect on the fretboard. If the layout seems familiar, it's probably because you've seen it before—in the E minor pentatonic scale patterns illustration in Fig. 37A (Chapter 5). Remember, every major pentatonic scale has a relative (shares the same notes) minor pentatonic counterpart (refer to "The Relative C Major Pentatonic Scale" section, earlier in this chapter). The G major pentatonic scale (G–A–B–D–E) shares the same notes as the E minor pentatonic scale (E–G–A–B–D); therefore, they are relative. As explained earlier, this means that they share the same scale patterns, but the roots are in different locations.

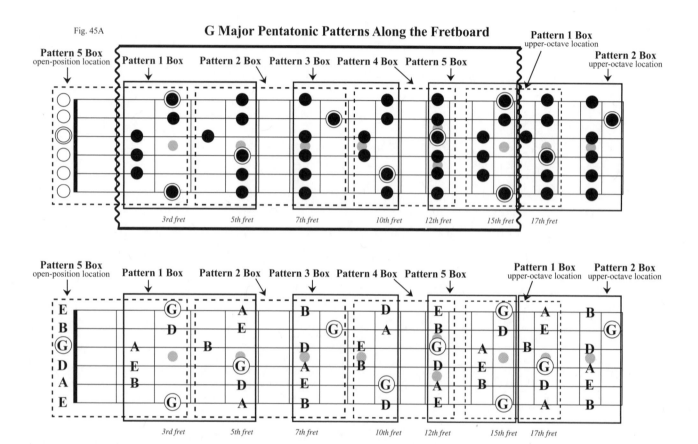

Fig. 45A — G Major Pentatonic Patterns Along the Fretboard

Fig. 45B is an exercise designed to help your ear tune in to the sound of the scale as you practice running through the patterns. Like the example in Fig. 41B, it focuses in on the "heart" notes of the scale: the root (G), 3rd (B), and the 5th (D).

🔊 TRACK 45

Fig. 45B

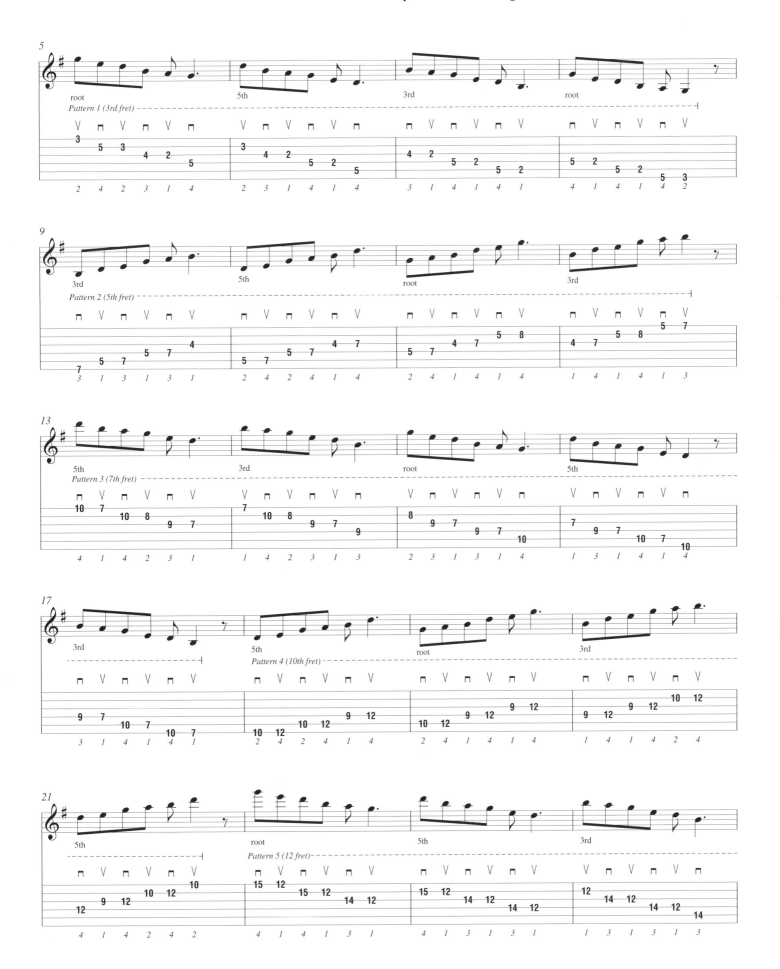

Connecting Pentatonic Patterns

Fig. 46A shows the five patterns of the D major pentatonic scale. Again, these patterns should look familiar. The D major pentatonic scale (D–E–F#–A–B) is relative to the B minor pentatonic scale (B–D–E–F#–A); therefore, they share the same scale patterns (with the roots adjusted, of course). Compare these pattern boxes with the ones in Fig. 39A (Chapter 5) to understand the correlation.

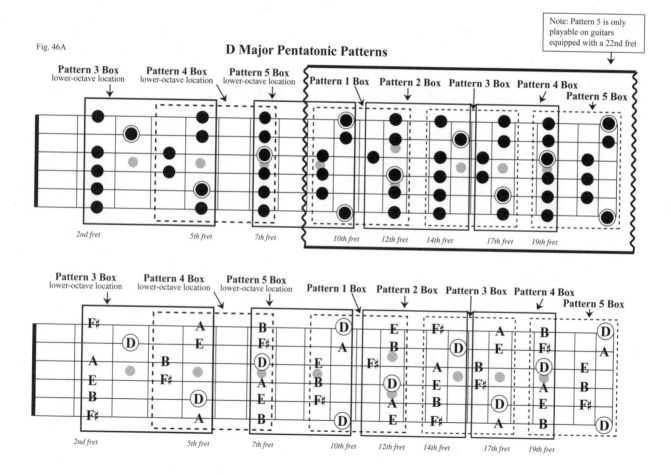

Fig. 46A

D Major Pentatonic Patterns

Note: Pattern 5 is only playable on guitars equipped with a 22nd fret

Fig. 46B is an exercise that will help you adjust your fingering to find the "heart" notes of the D major pentatonic patterns: D (root), F♯ (3rd), and A (5th).

TRACK 46

Fig. 46B

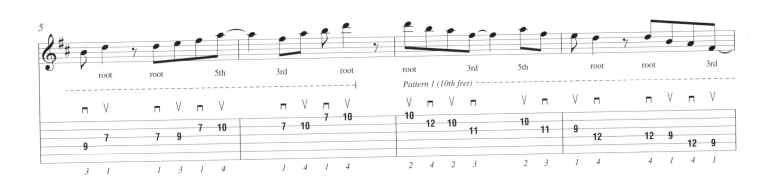

Solo 6C

Style: Southern Rock
Scales/Patterns:
>   G Major Pentatonic: Patterns 1, 2, 3, 4, and 5
>   C Major Pentatonic: Patterns 1, 2, 3, 4, and 5
>   D Major Pentatonic: Patterns 3, 4, and 5

Skill Level: Intermediate/Advanced

Solo 6C [**Fig. 47**] is in a "countrified" Southern rock vein. This is a style epitomized by the Allman Brothers Band, Marshall Tucker Band, the Outlaws, Lynyrd Skynyrd, and "border-crossing" bands such as the Doobie Brothers, Eagles, and the Grateful Dead. Influenced by the songs "Jessica" and "Ramblin' Man" by the Allman Brothers Band, the solo is highly indicative of Dickey Betts' pentatonic stylings. Spanning a total of 43 measures, it's the longest and one of the most challenging solos in this book. The sheer length, breakneck tempo (170 bpm), and frequent modulations are enough to send a fainthearted player running for the hills. But, as proven with the other solos in this book, when broken down and practiced in sections, little by little the task becomes much less daunting.

Though there appear to be a lot of chords in the progression, it's possible to simplify the harmonic "roadmap" in this manner—measures 1–8: key of G major; measures 9–12: C major; measures 13–16: G major; measures 17–20: D major; measures 21–24: C major; measures 25–43: G major. While the key centers are ever-shifting, the chord progressions within them stay pretty consistent. For example, discounting the passing Fadd9 chord (which is borrowed from the parallel key of G minor), measures 1–8 and 25–43 are simply a I–IV (G–Cadd9) vamp in the key of G major (refer to the chord frames at the top of the transcription). This I–IV theme is continued in the C major sections (measures 9–12 and 21–24), as well, in the guise of Cadd9–F6sus2. It can even be argued that the D major section (measures 17–20) follows the I–IV pattern, as well: D is the I chord, and Dsus2/4 suggests a G6/D (IV) chord quality. Here's one more suggestion for simplifying the progression: take another step back, view each section as containing a solitary I chord, and the whole arrangement bears resemblance to an elongated I–IV–V (G–C–D) blues progression!

G Major Introduction:

The solo opens in Pattern 3 of the G major pentatonic scale with a variation of the "fixed-string bend" lick from Fig. 26A (Chapter 4). Make sure you hold the B-string bend to pitch while attacking the high-E string notes. When you release the bend in measure 2, be sure to grab the next note (eighth fret, B string) with your middle (2nd) finger. This will put you in the "driver's seat" for the ensuing phrase (measures 2–3). The next phrase (measures 5–7) calls for the rollover technique (refer to Figs. 4F–G, Chapter 1) in a few spots. The first is at the juncture of measures 5 and 6, where the ring (3rd) finger has to grab the ninth-fret notes on the adjacent G and D strings. As an option, you could use your pinky to fret the G string notes, but you'd have to use a "hand scrunch" (see Fig. 19E, Chapter 3). The other rollover (measure 6) involves the index finger. Sorry, no options here. The last lick of this section contains an "open-string embellishment." A common country guitar maneuver, the procedure involves adding open-string attacks to your fretted licks, regardless of where you are playing on the fretboard.

The Shift to C Major:

Measure 9 heralds the C major modulation, and the solo makes a smooth transition to the C major pentatonic scale. The phrase starts with a low-range Pattern 4-to-Pattern 5 (lower-octave location) handoff maneuver and ends at the top of Pattern 1. This extended phrase (four measures) is basically the major counterpart to the extension box-assisted neck-climbing lick introduced in Fig. 9F (Chapter 1). Not particularly demanding from a fretboard aspect, the complexity of the passage lies in the rhythmic structure. The rhythmic "twist" occurs in measures 9 and 10, where the phrasing accents the downbeat of beats 1 and 4 of the first measure, and beat 3 of the next. This gives the groove a temporary 3/4 feel against the 4/4 meter. Rhythmic "recovery" doesn't take place until halfway through the section, at the top of measure 11.

Back to G:

At measure 13, it's back to the G major pentatonic scale, with some slippery maneuvers in Pattern 4. The rest of this passage (measures 14–16) requires subtle finesse. First, there's the double-slide move (see Figs. 5D–5F, Chapter 1) at the juncture of measures 14 and 15, followed by a series of descending slides on the G string, interspersed with fretted notes and open strings. If you stay faithful to the fingering and picking directions, you should be OK.

Enter D Major Pentatonic:

Measures 17–20 host a "guest appearance" by the D major pentatonic scale (see Fig. 46A), "flown in" specially to service the D and Dsus2/4 changes! This brief but crafty little passage journeys across the lower-octave locations of Patterns 3, 4, and 5. An open-D string attack launches the Pattern 3 phrase, which slides neatly into Pattern 4 (in measure 19) and, in turn, segues nicely into Pattern 5 (measure 20). Here are some things to watch out for: measures 17 and 18 employ the "3-against-4" feel that was introduced in measures 9 and 10 (measure 19 hints at this feel, as well); use your middle (2nd) finger to grab the fourth-fret G-string note at the end of measure 17, and prepare yourself for the rollover move in measure 19.

One More Time to C:

Measure 21 signals the final C major section. Here, the previous D major pentatonic phrase drops effortlessly into the overlapping (same area of the fretboard) Pattern 1 of the C major pentatonic scale. Beginning with a bend/release move, the phrase falls down the pattern and then segues to a double-slide maneuver on the G string in measure 22. This move kicks off a six-note melodic motif (see Fig. 8F, Chapter 1) that runs through measures 22–24, crossing the upper portions of Patterns 2, 3, and 4 along the way. The first three of these six-note groupings begin with a slide up the G string; the final one begins with a B-string slide and reaches fruition on the downbeat of measure 25. What's particularly intriguing about this passage is the offset nature of the motifs: they all start on an upbeat, rather than a downbeat.

Staying Put in G:

Measure 25 flags the final section, an extended outro in the key of G major. Here, the final note of the previous motif melds with the top note of Pattern 1 of the G major pentatonic scale (upper-octave location). Like a door hinge, the pivot note (a common-tone segue note belonging to both scales) "swings" immediately into a new phrase. Similar in structure to the lick in measure 21, it begins with a bend/release, followed by a fretted note on the same string. A B-string slide drops down into Pattern 5, where another bend/release move is mimicked by yet another in measure 26. This is followed by a set of pattern-juggling licks in measures 27–28 (follow the fingering suggestions carefully), capped with a low-E string *gliss* (rapid, extended slide) down the fretboard. Measure 29 starts a string-by-string climb that passes through sections of Patterns 1–4. The real star of this show, though, is the "3-against-4" feel of the passage. First introduced back in measures 9–10, here it runs full-tilt across a four-measure span! Be careful—it's easy to get lost in this "superimposed" meter. The placement of the last three notes (end of measure 32) should help to land you on your feet.

Measures 33–36 feature a cyclical ascension along the top two string set that targets the top note of Pattern 1 (upper-octave location). This can be a treacherous section due to the repetition and the potential rollover traps, where your fingers can get tied up in knots. Again, take it nice and slow and follow the fingering suggestions and picking directions carefully. Measure 37 starts a series of repetitive bends that, once again, suggest a 3/4 feel against the 4/4 groove. The last of these (end of measure 38) kicks off a modified "groups of 4" sequence that spills down into Pattern 5, where the solo culminates with a gradual G-string bend that is joined with a fixed-pitch note on the B string. Make sure that you bend the G string a whole step before striking the B-string note.

Tone Tips

Guitar: solidbody electric

Pickup Selection: neck and bridge

Pickup Type: humbuckers

Gain: 5

EQ: Bass/Middle/Treble: 4/7/6

Effects: moderate reverb (small hall)

Connecting Pentatonic Patterns

Fig. 47 "Solo 6C"

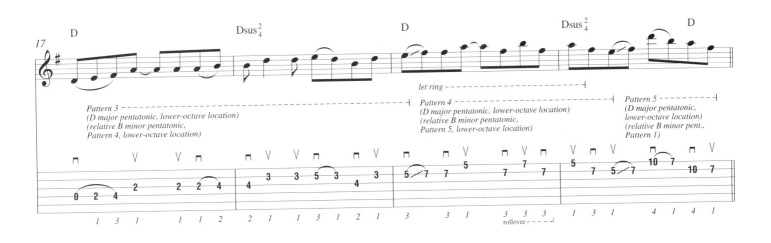

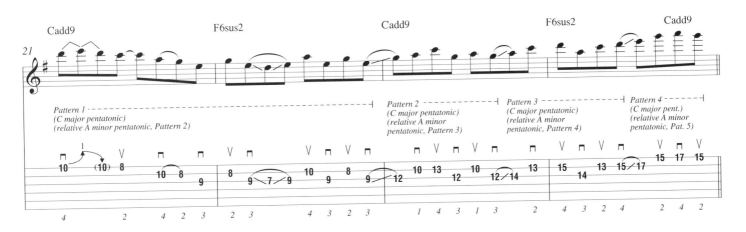

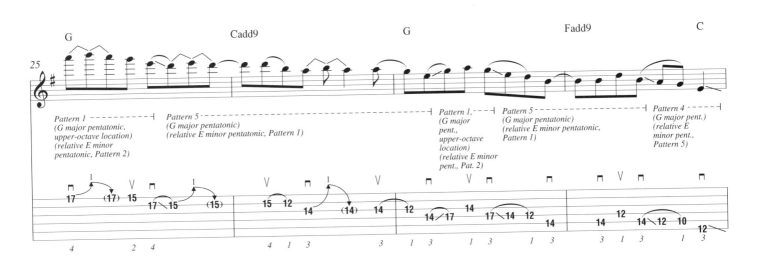

Connecting Pentatonic Patterns

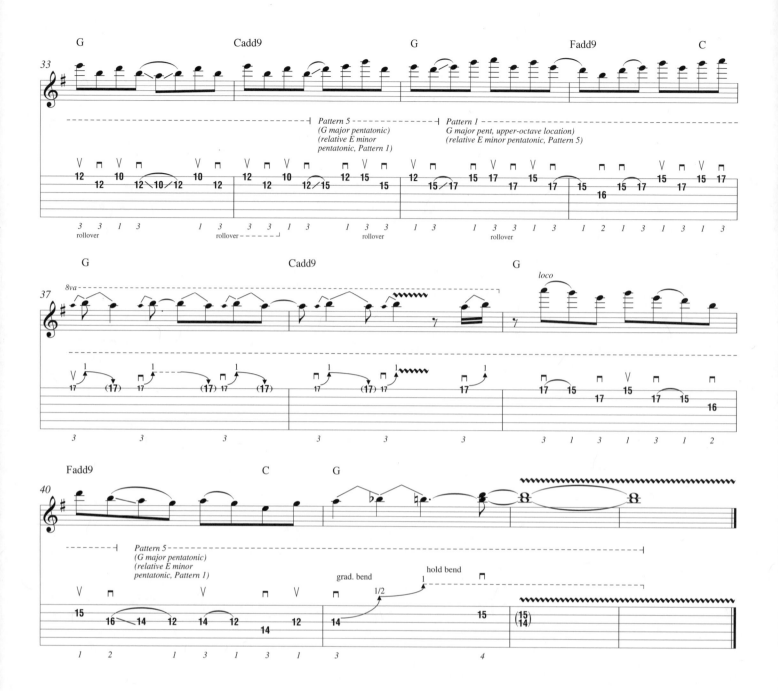

CHAPTER 7

COMBINING MAJOR AND MINOR PENTATONIC SCALES

Congratulations! You made it through the book! As a bonus, this chapter introduces a few more pentatonic applications for ongoing study. Aimed toward the intermediate-to-advanced player, it requires a working knowledge of all five patterns of both the major pentatonic and the minor pentatonic scale.

The Major/Minor Pentatonic Mix

It's common practice among experienced pentatonic players to overlap or combine parallel major and minor pentatonic scales (example: the A *major* pentatonic scale combined with the A *minor* pentatonic scale). Particularly useful over dominant seventh chords (root–3–5–♭7), it creates a major/minor "push-pull" sound that can inject a solo with blues-rock attitude or jazz-based sophistication. Some famous rock solos that display the major/minor mix include "Johnny B. Goode" by Chuck Berry, "Crossroads" by Cream, "Walk This Way" by Aerosmith, "Pride and Joy" by Stevie Ray Vaughan, "You Shook Me All Night Long" by AC/DC, and "Rock & Roll" by Led Zeppelin.

The main prerequisite for creating major/minor pentatonic licks is a keen awareness and understanding of overlapping *parallel* pentatonic scale patterns. "Parallel" means two different scales that share the same root. **Fig. 48A** on the following page shows two neck diagrams. The top diagram lines up the A major pentatonic scale patterns along the neck (some notes are not available in open position), while the bottom one depicts the *parallel* A minor pentatonic scale patterns. Let's compare Pattern 1 (at the fifth fret) of both scales. Both scales share the same root and 5th (A and E), but that's where the similarities end. Aside from the root and 5th, the major pentatonic scale contains the 2nd (B), 3rd (C♯), and 6th (F♯). By comparison, the minor pentatonic scale contains the ♭3rd (C), 4th (D), and ♭7th (G). Played back to back, they sound quite different indeed. But when the notes of the two scales are effectively combined, or "tossed around" like the ingredients of a great salad, the result is an intriguing dichotomy of "major/minor" dominant blues tonalities.

Connecting Pentatonic Patterns

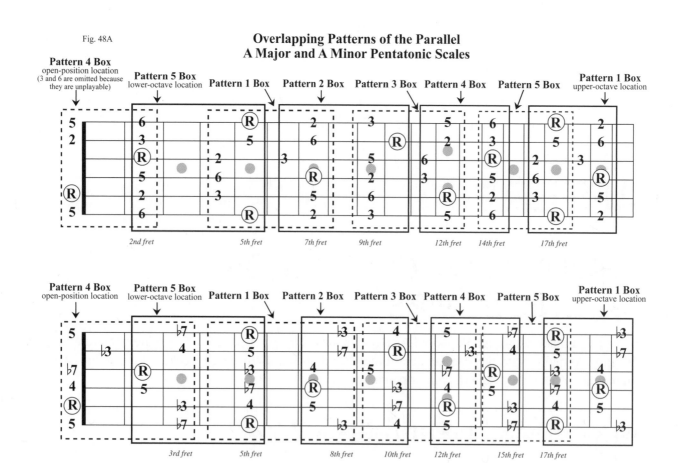

Fig. 48A

**Overlapping Patterns of the Parallel
A Major and A Minor Pentatonic Scales**

Before we get to the demonstration solo, wrap your fingers around the exercise in **Fig. 48B**. Purely a technical workout that trains your fingers to segue from scale to scale within each pattern, it will get you primed for the overlapping licks and phrases in the subsequent solo.

TRACK 48

Fig. 48B

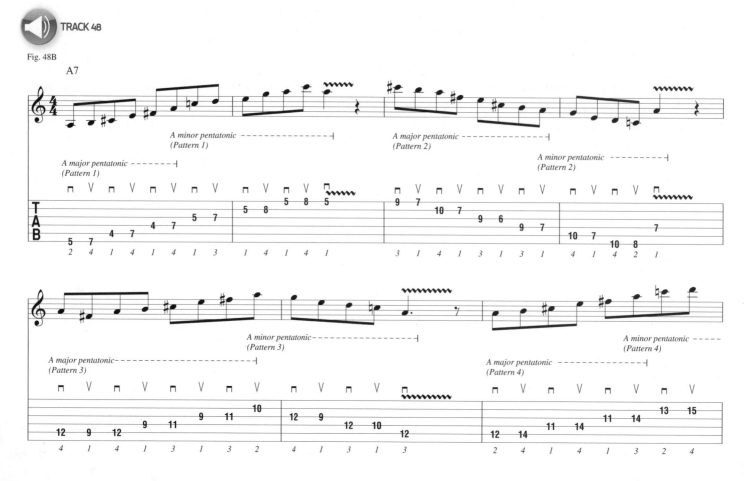

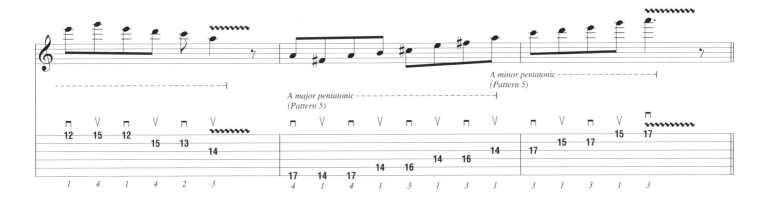

Solo 7A: Revisiting the 12-Bar Blues

Scales/Patterns:
> A Major Pentatonic: Patterns 1, 2, 3, 4, and 5
> A Minor Pentatonic: Patterns 1, 2, 3, 4, and 5
> E Major Pentatonic: Pattern 3
> E Minor Pentatonic: Pattern 3
> D Major Pentatonic: Pattern 4
> D Minor Pentatonic: Pattern 4

Skill Level: Intermediate/Advanced

For Solo 7A [**Fig. 49**], we're going to revisit the 12-bar dominant blues progression from Solos 2A and 2B. (For an explanation of the 12-bar system and dominant blues harmonies, refer back to Quick Theory Tutorials #3 and #4, in Chapter 2.) As you work your way through the solo, remember that all of the eighth notes are to receive the shuffle feel (see Fig. 4A, Chapter 1).

Measures 1–12: Major/Minor Pentatonic Madness and the Half-Step Bend:

Three-quarters of the progression involves the A7 chord, which makes for fertile ground while sewing A major/minor pentatonic licks over the musical landscape. The solo begins, right off the bat (pickup measure and measure 1), with a major/minor combination lick constructed from Pattern 1 of the A major and A minor pentatonic scales. (In the transcription, the overlapping patterns are referred to as "major/minor combination" patterns.) Notice the cohabitation of both the minor 3rd (C) and the major 3rd (C♯). This is the most significant factor that defines the major/minor tonality. In the pickup measure, the minor 3rd gives way to the major 3rd via a hammer-on maneuver, while in measure 1, a half-step bend handles the proceedings. Throughout the book, *quarter-step bends* have been employed liberally for the purpose of injecting "bluesy angst" to fretted minor 3rd notes (refer to Fig. 3E, Chapter 1). Here, with the *half-step bend*, the major-to-minor "rite of passage" is fully realized (refer to the scale tones notated above the music staff). Staying in Pattern 1, the next phrase (measure 2) employs a half-step bend/release to marry two different members of the parallel scales. The B note is the second degree (major 2nd) of the A *major* pentatonic scale; the C note is the ♭3rd (minor 3rd) of the A *minor* pentatonic scale. Viewing the first two licks as the "call-and-response" passage (refer to the solo analysis in Fig. 16, Chapter 2), the phrase in measures 3–4 is the "conclusion" phrase. Brimming with legato moves (note the rapid double pull-off maneuver in measure 3), it makes its way down Pattern 1 and nestles into the lower-octave location of Pattern 5 to greet the ensuing IV (D7) chord change. Beware of that "index-finger barre" half-step bend in measure 3! If you don't quite have the strength (or if your guitar is strung with heavy-gauge strings), you can substitute a hammer-on move instead (hammer on to the sixth fret of the G string with your middle finger).

Measure 5 brings the IV (D7) chord and the phrase picks up where the last one left off: a low F♯ note on the low-E string. Strategically placed, this note "nails the change" by hitting the 3rd of the chord (D7: D–F♯–A–C) just before the moment of impact (on the last note of the previous phrase). This leads to a snaky line that travels up Pattern 5 (the scale tones above the music staff still refer to the A major/minor combination scale) and slips into Pattern 1 at the last moments of measure 6. (Music theory note: with the exception of the grace note in measure 5, this D7 passage avoids the C♯, the major 3rd of the A major pentatonic scale. Some crafty players use this "omission" method to form Mixolydian phrases over the IV chord in dominant blues—in this case, D Mixolydian [D–E–F♯–G–A–B–C] over the D7 chord.) At measure 7, it's back to the I (A7) chord for more major/minor concoctions in Pattern 1. The end of measure 8 kicks off a cool, little A major pentatonic phrase that crosses Patterns 1 and 2 and tops off on the 12th fret of the B string on beat 4 of measure 9. (In terms of construction, this phrase is very similar to the minor pentatonic "neck-climbing" lick in Fig. 9F, Chapter 1.) Without taking a breath, this note is bent a half step (to C) and we're suddenly back in the major/minor mix. An intricate Pattern 3 "combo" lick ensues (juncture of measures 9 and 10), followed by some fancy A-string maneuvering (end of measure 10), and the first "chorus" (one time through the 12-bar form) goes out with a classic "turnaround phrase" (see Measures 1–12 analysis of Solo 2A, Chapter 2) crafted from Patterns 4 and 3. In regard to these last few licks (measures 9–12), fret-hand fingering is of the utmost importance! Put the passages together slowly and carefully before trying to play them up to tempo.

Measures 13–24: "The Caveman Meets the Sophisticated Gentleman":

The second chorus starts out with a bang! The section opens with a quirky but aggressive lick that travels up through Patterns 3 and 4 (note the chromatic passage along the B string), and segues immediately to a relentlessly cycled "fixed-string bend" (see Fig. 19G, Chapter 3) double-stop figure. Rich in harmonic overtones, this bent dyad is one of the staples of the "aggressive" blues genre. Diving down to Pattern 2, a potent string-rake figure (rapidly strummed chord shape) kicks off a tricky passage that zips across Patterns 1 and 5 (lower-octave location) and bottoms out in Pattern 4 (open-position location).

At this point, the solo takes on an aggressive nature that's more primal than it is cerebral. An open-position phrase pounds the low-E string into submission (top of measure 16) before shifting to a series of inverted power chords (see Fig. 31C, Chapter 5) that are served up with heavy downpicked attacks. (An important right-hand dynamic, downpicking can add considerable power and authority to your lead playing.) Energy is still the key factor when the IV (D7) chord arrives in measure 17. Not a lot of thought process here; just a rhythmic series of 4ths dyads on the top string set (see Fig. 10K, Chapter 1), interspersed with some G-string punctuations. You may need to be a caveman to perform the double-stop bends in measure 18! The quarter-step bends aren't so scary, but you'll need to dig into the fretboard to raise both the B and the high-E string a half step. As an alternative, you may want to cast away one of those notes and just bend the high-E string, or the B string.

Measures 19 and 20 mark the juncture where brain meets brawn. Here, the phrasing shifts to a series of "harmonic intervals" (see Quick Theory Tutorial #2, Chapter 1) played along the G and B strings. Here's some clarification for what can be a confusing passage: begin by planting your index finger on the eighth fret of the B string and your middle finger on the ninth fret of the G string. Now move the dyad shape up two frets. Next, move it up to the 13th fret, and, finally, to the 17th fret. These are the four fretboard moves involved in the entire passage. The rest is just picking accuracy.

At measure 21, sophistication moves in with an "uptown" blues lick cast from Pattern 3 of the E major/minor pentatonic combination scale. (Refer to the neck diagrams in Fig. 48A: move the Pattern 3 boxes up the fretboard so that the roots align with the E notes on the A and B strings.) Not particularly "note-y," but it outlines the E7 chord change in a bluesy fashion. The D7 lick uses similar tactics. It's drawn from Pattern 4 of the D major/minor pentatonic combination scale. (Refer to the neck diagrams in Fig. 48A: move the Pattern 4 boxes up the neck to align the roots with D notes on the A and G strings.) Be careful—this pattern is very similar to Pattern 1 of the A major/minor pentatonic combination scale used throughout this solo. It can be easy to get them mixed up. Brawn comes in to play again in the final two measures, where a ferocious lick tumbles down the fretboard through Patterns 4, 3, and 2.

Tone Tips

Guitar: solidbody electric

Pickup Selection: neck

Pickup Type: single coil

Gain: 7

EQ: Bass/Middle/Treble: 3/9/8

Effects: moderate reverb (small room)

TRACK 49

Fig. 49 "Solo 7A"

♩ = 110 (♪♪ = ♪³♪)

R = root of both scales
2nd = 2nd degree of the major pentatonic scale
♭3rd = ♭3rd of the minor pentatonic scale
3rd = 3rd of the major pentatonic scale
4th = 4th of the minor pentatonic scale
5th = 5th of both scales
6th = 6th of the major pentatonic scale
♭7th = ♭7th of the minor pentatonic scale

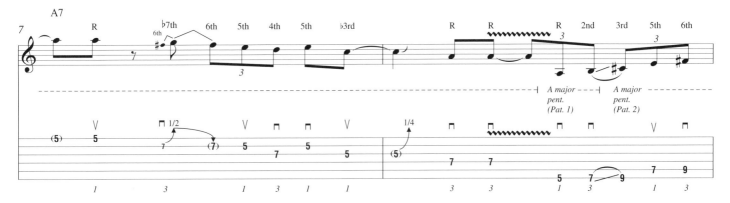

Connecting Pentatonic Patterns

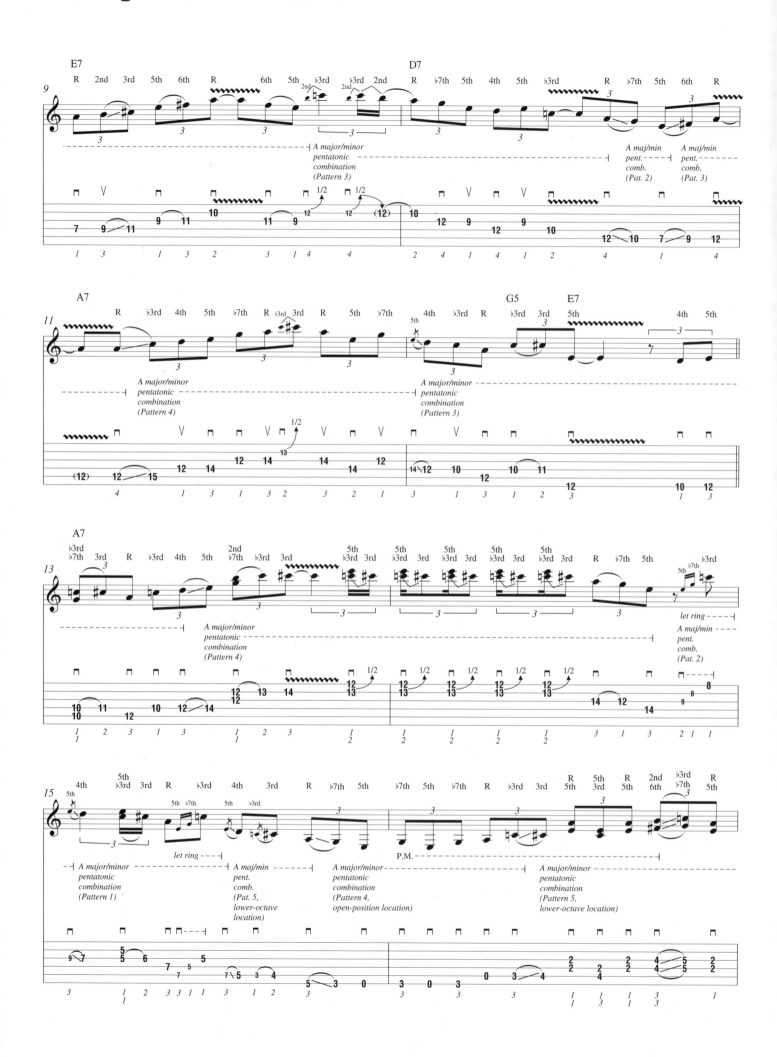

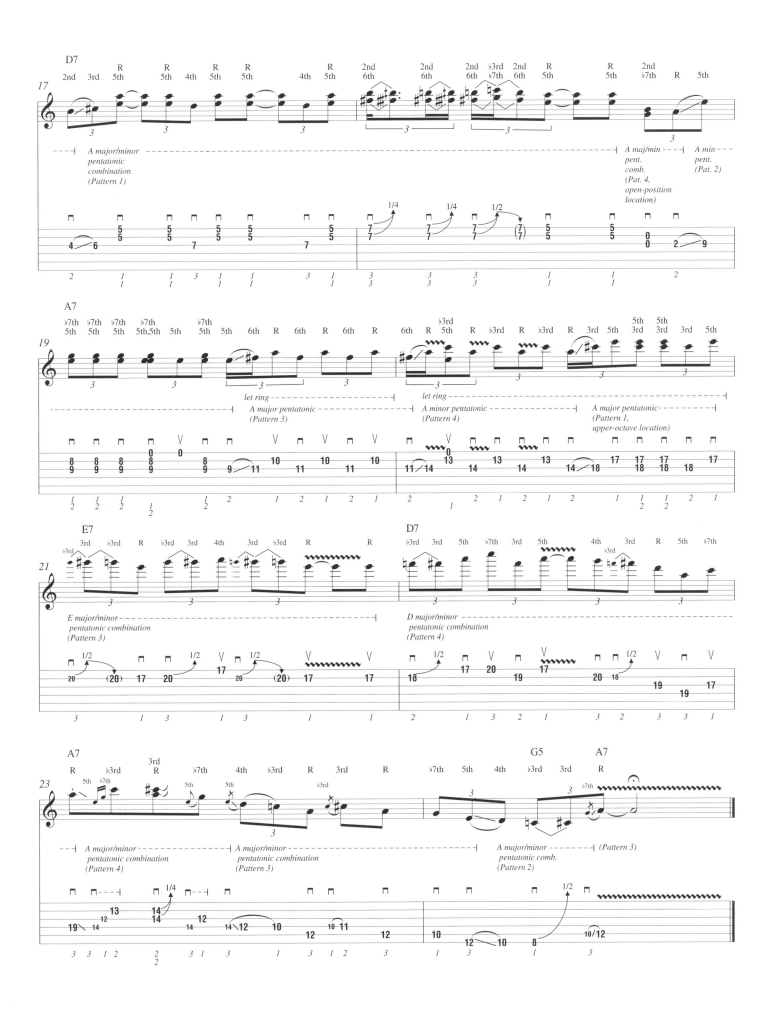

Minor Pentatonic Substitution

Many players get extra mileage out of their minor pentatonic licks simply by transporting them to different areas of the fretboard. Essentially, this is the same as transposing to a different key, but this transferal can sometimes work even while the band "stays put" on a solitary chord. For example, the band might be chugging away on an Am chord (A–C–E) while the guitarist plays a collection of A minor pentatonic phrases interspersed with B minor pentatonic and E minor pentatonic licks. Some players who specialize in this "pentatonic stew" are Eric Johnson, Larry Carlton, Jeff Beck, Robby Krieger (the Doors), and Scott Henderson (Tribal Tech).

The applications of *pentatonic substitution* are boundless and only limited to the player's imagination. Consequently, a study of the topic is well beyond the scope of this book (for more on pentatonic substitution and pentatonic variations, see the suggested companion book *Soloing Strategies* [Hal Leonard]), but for starters, here's one of the most common techniques: it involves partnering your favorite minor pentatonic pattern with its "twin pattern" two frets above. For example, say the band is playing an Em or Em7 chord, and you're soloing in Pattern 1 of the E minor pentatonic scale at the 12th fret. As an experiment, or by accident, you move a portion of one of your "pet" phrases up two frets, to Pattern 1 of the F♯ minor pentatonic scale, and it sounds good to you—especially if you "resolve" back to the E minor pentatonic scale pattern [**Fig. 50A–B**]. Essentially, you just employed pentatonic substitution; in this case, *diatonic substitution* within the E Dorian mode. That's fancy talk for "playing all of the notes of the E Dorian scale (E–F♯–G–A–B–C♯–D) by using only minor pentatonic patterns."

Without getting too bogged down with traditional music theory, let's just view this topic as a way to experiment and expand your pentatonic vocabulary. That said, let's move along to the final solo in this book.

"Pet" E Minor Pentatonic Phrase (variation of Fig. 3E in Chapter 1)

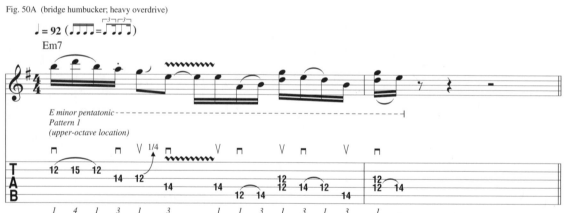

Fig. 50A (bridge humbucker; heavy overdrive)

Second Portion of the "Pet" Phrase Transported to F♯ Minor Pentatonic

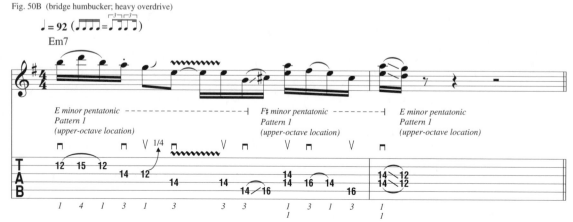

Fig. 50B (bridge humbucker; heavy overdrive)

Solo 7B: E Minor Jam Using Pentatonic Substitution

Scales/Patterns:

      E Minor Pentatonic: Patterns 1, 2, 3, 4, and 5

      F♯ Minor Pentatonic: Patterns 1, 2, 3, 4, and 5

      B Minor Pentatonic: Pattern 1

      A Minor Pentatonic: Patterns 1 and 5

      E♭, D, D♭, and C Minor Pentatonic: Pattern 1 for Each

Skill Level: Intermediate/Advanced

Solo 7B [**Fig. 51**] is a funky jam over an Em7 chord (E–G–B–D). Similar to the solo in Fig. 38 (Solo 5C), this solo uses the E minor pentatonic scale to build the foundation of the phrases. But, as you'll see, it's also strewn with pentatonic substitution applications.

Establishing an E Dorian Theme:

The solo opens with a low-E string *gliss* from the 12th fret, followed by an open low-E string attack. What follows is a string of tradeoffs between neighboring patterns of E minor and F♯ minor pentatonic. These tradeoffs consist of only two notes from each pattern, but the pairs are all launched with the open low-E, A, and D string attacks. (Technically, all of the open strings "belong" to Pattern 1 of the E minor pentatonic scale.) Even though the lines are simple, they're enough to tell the listener that there's something more going on here than just E minor pentatonic. At the end of measure 2, the tradeoffs jump higher up the neck, to neighboring Pattern 1 positions (upper-octave location) of the two pentatonic scales. (The contour of these lines is very distinct and works well if you follow the legato markings carefully.) With the introduction of the C♯ note at the end of measure 2, the E Dorian mode (E–F♯–G–A–B–C♯–D) is in full swing, and the main "theme" of the solo is established. The end of measure 4 takes us further up the neck, to neighboring Pattern 2 patterns of E and F♯ minor pentatonic. These slippery figures lead to a highly syncopated line (measure 6), played out between Pattern 1 boxes again. Fireworks follow in measure 7, where a hammer-on/adjacent-string sequence (see Fig. 27E, Chapter 4) shoots up the symmetrical pattern pictured above the notation staff in the transcription. This very handy quasi-scale pattern is constructed from the lower (toward the headstock) notes of Pattern 1 of E minor pentatonic and Pattern 1 of F♯ minor pentatonic. Although the scale tones aren't in consecutive order (thus the term, "quasi"), every note of E Dorian is incorporated in this supremely finger-friendly pattern.

Mixing in More Pentatonic Scales:

Measure 9 goes back to mid-neck with a funky melody cast from Pattern 3 of the E minor pentatonic. The next measure mimics the contour of the melody, but in Pattern 1 of B minor pentatonic. B minor pentatonic can be a great substitute for E minor pentatonic because all of the notes are relative—except for the F♯, which, in many cases, is a pleasing, melodic addition. The copycat tradeoff lines build to a climax in measure 11 (Pattern 4 of E minor pentatonic and Pattern 1 of B minor pentatonic), setting the stage for the A minor pentatonic frenzy (Pattern 1) of measure 12. The combination of all the notes of E minor, B minor, and A minor pentatonic produces the E natural minor (or E Aeolian) scale: E–F♯–G–A–B–C–D. A minor pentatonic can be a useful substitution scale, but it should be used with caution. Try to avoid starting or ending phrases with the scale's C note, as that note can clash with chords and chord progressions in certain situations.

Back to Dorian, Followed by a Step "Outside":

Measure 13 marks a return to the E Dorian theme and the riff-like structure of the beginning of the solo. Diving down to the low E again, the E minor and F♯ minor pentatonic tradeoffs commence with Pattern 1 swapping (measure 13), followed by Pattern 3 handoffs (measure 14) and some Pattern 5 and Pattern 1 dance moves in measures 14 and 15. Measure 16 rides a captivating "dotted-eighth/16th-note" rhythmic-motif figure that walks up Pattern 1 of F♯ minor pentatonic. This is answered by an attitude-filled E minor pentatonic phrase that spills from Pattern 2 down into Pattern 1 (upper-octave locations). The closing measures push pentatonic substitution to the "outside" limit with a quirky three-note figure that snakes its way down the fretboard in chromatic increments (one fret at a time). The lesson here is that any note on the fretboard can be made to work at any given time in a solo (even notes that are "outside" the key center, like the ones in this passage). The rule is: you need to have direction and purpose when you intersperse "questionable" notes in a solo. For instance, this chromatic passage is bookended by solid E minor pentatonic licks. The "outside" segment springs from consonance, travels through dissonance, and slips back into the tonal pocket at the end of the mayhem.

Tone Tips

Guitar: solidbody electric

Pickup Selection: bridge

Pickup Type: humbucker

Gain: 8

EQ: Bass/Middle/Treble: 3/10/6

Effects: moderate reverb (bright hall)

TRACK 51

Fig. 51 "Solo 7B"

CHAPTER 8

JAM TRACKS WITH SOLOING SUGGESTIONS

Welcome to the "Jam Tracks" chapter. Here, you will find chord charts for some of the progressions used in this book. Backing tracks for all of these progressions are included with the audio (Tracks 52–57). These tracks are in "extended form," so you'll have accompaniment as you improvise your own solos.

To help you get started "jamming," each chord chart includes pentatonic scale suggestions notated below the staff. The suggestions are grouped into three levels of difficulty: Beginner, Intermediate, and Advanced. The Beginner level is directed towards players who are just starting to connect pentatonic patterns on the fretboard. The intermediate level is for those who can grasp the concepts brought forth in the book, but need to practice applying them. The advanced level is for experienced soloists looking for ways to expand their pentatonic prowess. Pentatonic substitution (see Chapter 7) is often used as a tactic in this category.

Choose the level that best describes your playing experience, and dive in! That said, you don't necessarily have to follow the scale suggestions. For instance, you could use the backing tracks to practice various licks and solos in the book, or you may even choose to ignore the directions and just start moving your fingers on the fretboard to see what you can come up with. In any case, the main objective is to have fun!

Jam Progression 1: Hard Rock Ballad

The first progression [**Fig. 52**] is a hard rock ballad in the key of A minor. This is the progression used for Solos 1A and 1B. (For an explanation of the key center and the progression, refer to the solo analysis in Fig. 11, Chapter 1.) The letter "A" marks the first eight-measure section, which is played twice. The B section is another eight-measure section, but it is played only once. The entire form is repeated, but with an alternate ending for the B section (the Coda).

If you need to look up scale patterns, here's a listing of where you can find them in this book:

A Minor Pentatonic, Patterns 1–5: Fig. 32A, Chapter 5

E Minor Pentatonic, Patterns 1–5: Fig. 37A, Chapter 5

B Minor Pentatonic, Patterns 1–5: Fig. 39A, Chapter 5

D Minor Pentatonic, Patterns 1–4: Fig. 27I, Chapter 4

F♯ Minor Pentatonic, Pattern 1: Fig. 40 (measure 9), Chapter 5

C Major Pentatonic, Patterns 1–5: Fig. 41A, Chapter 6

G Major Pentatonic, Patterns 1–5: Fig. 45A, Chapter 6

D Major Pentatonic, Patterns 1–5: Fig. 46A, Chapter 6

A Major Pentatonic, Patterns 1–5: Fig. 48A, Chapter 7

Major/Minor Pentatonic Combination Scale Patterns: Fig. 48A, Chapter 7

Connecting Pentatonic Patterns

 TRACK 52

Fig. 52 "Jam Track 1"

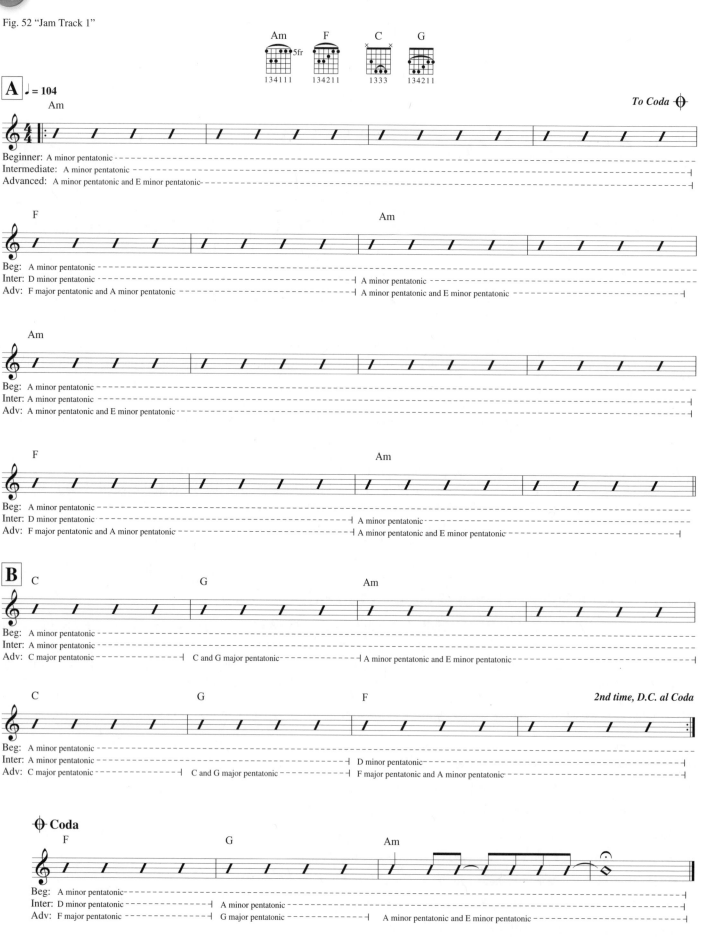

Jam Progression 2: Dominant Blues Shuffle

Fig. 53 is the 12-bar blues progression used in Solos 2A, 2B, and 7A. (For an analysis of the progression, refer to Fig. 16, Chapter 2.) In this extended version, the band plays four choruses (four times through the form), giving you plenty of breathing space to practice your licks and phrases.

TRACK 53

Fig. 53 "Jam Track 2"

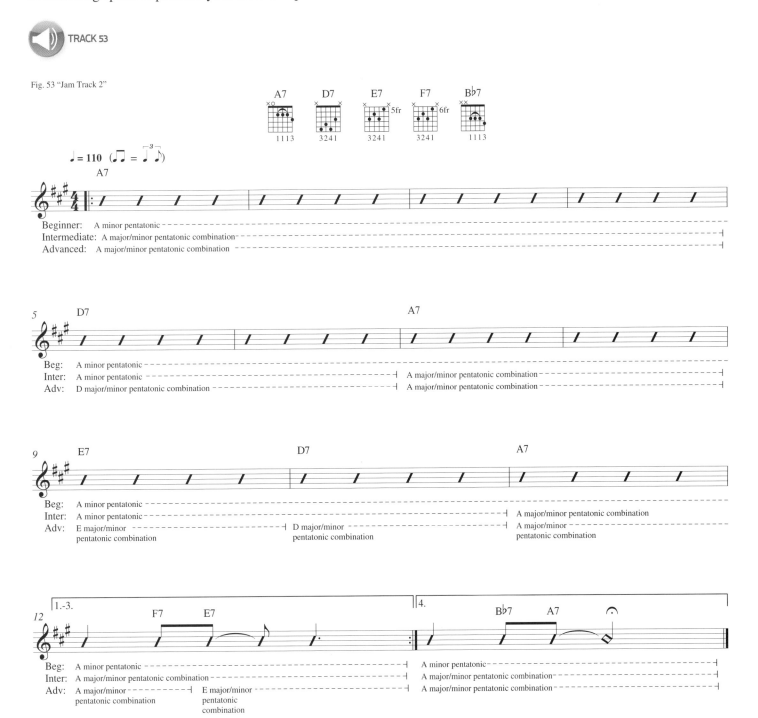

Jam Progression 3: Uptempo Hard Rock

Jam Track 3 [**Fig. 54**] is a fast rocker that modulates back and forth from A minor to D minor (refer to Fig. 27I in Chapter 4 for patterns of the D minor pentatonic scale). Based on the progression used for Solos 4A and 4B in Chapter 4 (refer to Fig. 28 in Chapter 4 for analysis of the progression), this version is much longer, giving you time to really stretch out.

TRACK 54

Fig. 54 "Jam Track 3"

Jam Progression 4: "Hip-Hop" Funk Rock

Jam Track 4 [**Fig. 55**] is a funk rock jam over an Em7 chord (E–G–B–D) vamp. "Hip-hop" means that the 16th-note rhythms are shuffled (refer to Fig. 38 in Chapter 5). For beginners and intermediate players, see what you can come up with as you practice "putting the neck together" with E minor pentatonic scale patterns (refer to 37A, Chapter 5). Advanced players can really stretch out and test the bounds of pentatonic substitution (see Chapter 7).

TRACK 55

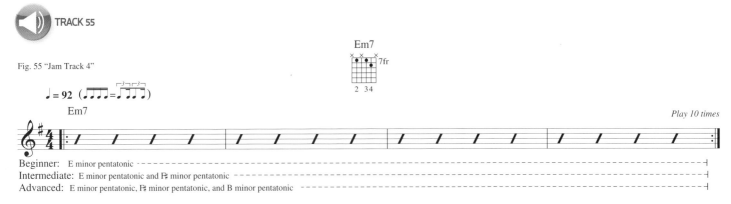

Fig. 55 "Jam Track 4"

Jam Progression 5: Minor Blues Ballad

Fig. 56 is a slow minor blues. Very similar to the progression used in Solo 5D, this one stays truer to the 12-bar form (see solo analysis in Fig. 40, Chapter 5). A word to the advanced players: the pentatonic scale suggestions (B, E, and F♯ minor) for the Bm7 (i) chord can be combined to create B Aeolian (B–C♯–D–E–F♯–G–A, also called the "B natural minor scale") melodies (refer to "Minor Pentatonic Substitution" in Chapter 7).

TRACK 56

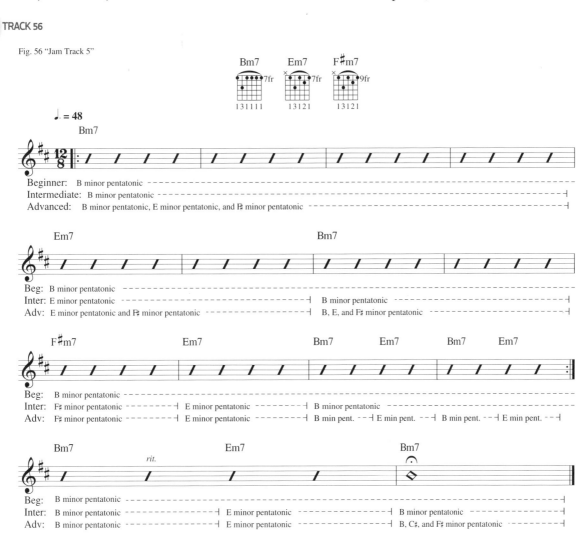

Fig. 56 "Jam Track 5"

Jam Progression 6: Major Key Southern Rock

Jam Progression 6 [**Fig. 57**] is an Allman Brothers-style outing with modulating major key centers. Although the form is much longer here, it's basically the same progression used for Solo 6C (see the chord progression analysis in Fig. 47, Chapter 6). Beginners, if you're still struggling with major pentatonic scales, you can use relative minor pentatonic scale patterns (refer to the opening paragraphs of Chapter 6).

TRACK 57

Fig. 57 "Jam Track 6"

GUITAR NOTATION LEGEND

Guitar music can be notated three different ways: on a *musical staff*, in *tablature*, and in *rhythm slashes*.

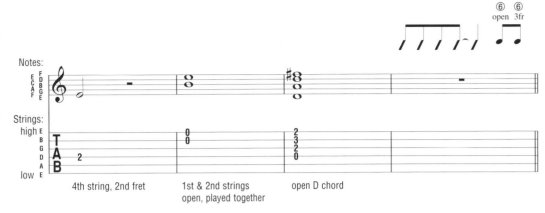

RHYTHM SLASHES are written above the staff. Strum chords in the rhythm indicated. Use the chord diagrams found at the top of the first page of the transcription for the appropriate chord voicings. Round noteheads indicate single notes.

THE MUSICAL STAFF shows pitches and rhythms and is divided by bar lines into measures. Pitches are named after the first seven letters of the alphabet.

TABLATURE graphically represents the guitar fingerboard. Each horizontal line represents a string, and each number represents a fret.

Definitions for Special Guitar Notation

HALF-STEP BEND: Strike the note and bend up 1/2 step.

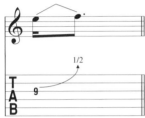

BEND AND RELEASE: Strike the note and bend up as indicated, then release back to the original note. Only the first note is struck.

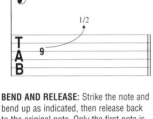

VIBRATO: The string is vibrated by rapidly bending and releasing the note with the fretting hand.

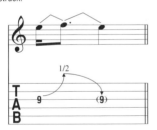

LEGATO SLIDE: Strike the first note and then slide the same fret-hand finger up or down to the second note. The second note is not struck.

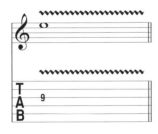

WHOLE-STEP BEND: Strike the note and bend up one step.

PRE-BEND: Bend the note as indicated, then strike it.

WIDE VIBRATO: The pitch is varied to a greater degree by vibrating with the fretting hand.

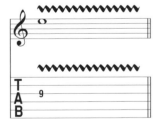

SHIFT SLIDE: Same as legato slide, except the second note is struck.

GRACE NOTE BEND: Strike the note and immediately bend up as indicated.

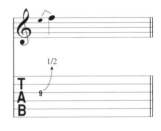

PRE-BEND AND RELEASE: Bend the note as indicated. Strike it and release the bend back to the original note.

HAMMER-ON: Strike the first (lower) note with one finger, then sound the higher note (on the same string) with another finger by fretting it without picking.

TRILL: Very rapidly alternate between the notes indicated by continuously hammering on and pulling off.

SLIGHT (MICROTONE) BEND: Strike the note and bend up 1/4 step.

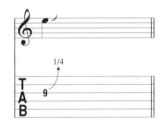

UNISON BEND: Strike the two notes simultaneously and bend the lower note up to the pitch of the higher.

PULL-OFF: Place both fingers on the notes to be sounded. Strike the first note and without picking, pull the finger off to sound the second (lower) note.

TAPPING: Hammer ("tap") the fret indicated with the pick-hand index or middle finger and pull off to the note fretted by the fret hand.

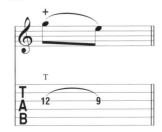

NATURAL HARMONIC: Strike the note while the fret-hand lightly touches the string directly over the fret indicated.

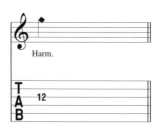

PINCH HARMONIC: The note is fretted normally and a harmonic is produced by adding the edge of the thumb or the tip of the index finger of the pick hand to the normal pick attack.

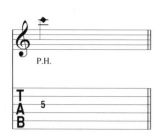

HARP HARMONIC: The note is fretted normally and a harmonic is produced by gently resting the pick hand's index finger directly above the indicated fret (in parentheses) while the pick hand's thumb or pick assists by plucking the appropriate string.

PICK SCRAPE: The edge of the pick is rubbed down (or up) the string, producing a scratchy sound.

MUFFLED STRINGS: A percussive sound is produced by laying the fret hand across the string(s) without depressing, and striking them with the pick hand.

PALM MUTING: The note is partially muted by the pick hand lightly touching the string(s) just before the bridge.

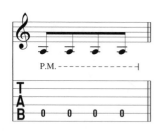

RAKE: Drag the pick across the strings indicated with a single motion.

TREMOLO PICKING: The note is picked as rapidly and continuously as possible.

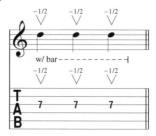

ARPEGGIATE: Play the notes of the chord indicated by quickly rolling them from bottom to top.

VIBRATO BAR DIVE AND RETURN: The pitch of the note or chord is dropped a specified number of steps (in rhythm), then returned to the original pitch.

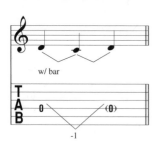

VIBRATO BAR SCOOP: Depress the bar just before striking the note, then quickly release the bar.

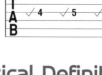

VIBRATO BAR DIP: Strike the note and then immediately drop a specified number of steps, then release back to the original pitch.

Additional Musical Definitions

(accent)
- Accentuate note (play it louder).

(accent)
- Accentuate note with great intensity.

(staccato)
- Play the note short.

- Downstroke

V
- Upstroke

D.S. al Coda
- Go back to the sign (𝄋), then play until the measure marked "*To Coda*," then skip to the section labelled "Coda."

D.C. al Fine
- Go back to the beginning of the song and play until the measure marked "*Fine*" (end).

Rhy. Fig.
- Label used to recall a recurring accompaniment pattern (usually chordal).

Riff
- Label used to recall composed, melodic lines (usually single notes) which recur.

Fill
- Label used to identify a brief melodic figure which is to be inserted into the arrangement.

Rhy. Fill
- A chordal version of a Fill.

tacet
- Instrument is silent (drops out).

- Repeat measures between signs.

- When a repeated section has different endings, play the first ending only the first time and the second ending only the second time.

NOTE: Tablature numbers in parentheses mean:
1. The note is being sustained over a system (note in standard notation is tied), or
2. The note is sustained, but a new articulation (such as a hammer-on, pull-off, slide or vibrato) begins, or
3. The note is a barely audible "ghost" note (note in standard notation is also in parentheses).